Everything You Need to Know to
LOSE WEIGHT AND HAVE FUN
at the Same Time

MALL
WALKING
MADNESS

SARA DONOVAN
Founder of Walk-Sport **America**
WITH GARY LEGWOLD

RODALE

© 2002 by Sara Donovan and Gary Legwold

All rights reserved. No part of this publication may be reproduced or transmitted in any form or by any means, electronic or mechanical, including photocopying, recording, or any other information storage and retrieval system, without the written permission of the publisher.

Printed in the United States of America
Rodale Inc. makes every effort to use acid-free ∞, recycled paper ♻.

Photographs by Mitch Mandel/Rodale Images

Interior and cover design by Tara Long
Cover photograph by Thomas Perry
Cover illustration by Carl Mazer

Library of Congress Cataloging-in-Publication Data

Donovan, Sara.
    Mall walking madness : everything you need to know to lose weight and
have fun at the same time / Sara Donovan, with Gary Legwold.
        p.   cm.
    Includes index.
    ISBN 1–57954–614–5 paperback
    1. Fitness walking.   2. Shopping malls.   I. Legwold, Gary.   II. Title.
RA781.65 .D665 2002
613.7'176—dc21   2002006883

Distributed to the book trade by St. Martin's Press

2   4   6   8   10   9   7   5   3   1   paperback

RODALE

WE **INSPIRE** AND **ENABLE** PEOPLE TO IMPROVE
THEIR LIVES AND THE WORLD AROUND THEM

FOR MORE OF OUR PRODUCTS
WWW.RODALESTORE.COM
(800) 848-4735

Contents

Acknowledgments

Nobody accomplishes anything big alone.

I have been blessed with outstanding people in my life who have given me magnificent direction and support for this book. They are smart, generous, cool, kind, creative, and somewhat pushy people. In other words: they challenge me—*wonderfully*.

I dare not attempt to name each and every individual person who has helped me on this path. I would undoubtedly forget one of you, and then remember you as soon as the ink dries on the presses!

You know who you are. *I thank you from the bottom and top of my heart.*

I would also like to acknowledge a notable group of people: the Mall Stars! of Mall of America. This group of diehards is the one that catapulted me into the mall walking world. They feed my ongoing passion and belief that mall walking is one of the greatest ways to improve one's health and outlook on life. They are a class act. In large part, it was these people who taught me that walking is as fun as the person that you are walking with, that there is *no* excuse not to do it, and walking in a mall is "where it's at" for those who are committed to exercise. After all, health clubs don't have J.C. Penney, Nordstrom, or the Gap!

Finally I would like to acknowledge the three most important people in my life:

Tara, Peter, and George.

Thank you for your strength, for the essential lessons you teach me, for your love, and for being so unbelievably fun and funny.

You are my first creations, and my best.

—Sara Donovan

The publisher wishes to acknowledge the following organizations for granting permission to reprint their materials in this book.

The "Rate Your Diet" test on page 74 © 1996, CSPI. Reprinted/adapted from *Nutrition Action Healthletter*, published by the Center for Science in the Public Interest (CSPI), 1875 Connecticut Ave., N.W., Suite 300, Washington, DC 20009-5728. $24.00 for 10 issues.

The PAR-Q on page 83 is reprinted from the 1994 revised version of the Physical Activity Readiness Questionnaire (PAR-Q and YOU). PAR-Q and YOU is a copyrighted, pre-exercise screen owned by the Canadian Society for Exercise Physiology.

The Modified Sit-and-Reach Test (text only) on page 87 is reprinted by permission from the American College of Sports Medicine, 1998, *ACSM Fitness Book*, second edition (Champaign, IL: Human Kinetics), 36–37.

The Modified Sit-and-Reach Test (table only) on page 88 is reprinted by permission from S. Blair et al.: *ACSM Resource Manual for Guidelines for Exercise Testing & Prescription*, 1988, Spec. Matl: Sit-and-Reach Table Page 165 (Philadelphia: Lea & Febiger, imprint of Lippincott Williams & Wilkins).

The arthritis information on pages 211 and 212 © 2002. Reprinted with permission of the Arthritis Foundation 1330 W. Peachtree St., Atlanta, GA 30309. To order a free copy of the *Exercise and Your Arthritis* or *Diet and Your Arthritis* brochures, please call the Arthritis Foundation's Information Line at (800) 283-7800 or log on to www.arthritis.org.

Dairy Queen® is a registered trademark of the American Dairy Queen Corporation.

TCBY® is a registered trademark of TCBY Enterprises.

Introduction

When I speak about the WalkSport program at mall walking clubs around the country, hundreds of people come out, bubbling over to learn about mall walking. Now, I could pretend they're there to hear me talk about weight management, fitness, and other health topics, but the truth is, they're probably there because they've heard the rumor that has turned mall walking into a movement that's sweeping the nation: Mall walking is *fun*.

Many of them have started other fitness and weight loss programs for very real reasons: They wanted to lose weight, or lower their blood pressure, or help control their blood sugar. While their intentions and motivations may have been good, they found themselves dropping out or giving up, because their workouts just felt like *work*. But standing in a group together, they find themselves surrounded by mall walking's secret weapon: buddies.

You gain a lot of pals with mall walking. The mall walkers who *keep* coming day after day do so because of a buddy system of other mall walkers. We pull each other along, learn from each other as we walk, and motivate each other to stick with it.

This social aspect of mall walking is not to be taken lightly. It is the major reason mall walkers stay with their exercise program long after people who do other activities hang it up. I know that when I mall walk, I feel good about me—and it shows. My muscles are loose and strong, I'm on the move, and I'm upbeat about life. I can see other mall walkers feel this way, and we can't help picking up on each other's good vibes.

Take my friend John, for example. I call him "the Robin Williams of mall walking," and this comedic streak has already netted him a big score—John actually courted his wife, Esther, while they were mall walking. I can walk with John for, oh, 5 seconds and already he's into a joke. He seems to have one for every situation—this is his walking joke:

1

"This guy's wife is not receptive to his hugging," says John. "He goes to the doc, who advises him to walk 10 miles per week. Then his wife will hug him. So, 7 weeks pass and the doc gets a call from this guy.

"'How are things between you and your wife?' asks the doc.

"'I don't know,' says the guy, 'I'm 70 miles away from home.'"

When you're treated to this kind of entertainment from a mall walking buddy, it's not hard to understand how you can stick with your program so faithfully. When Judy walks with her buddy, Pat, at the Mayfair Mall in Wauwatosa, Wisconsin, Judy swears, "our mouths go faster than our feet."

As we walk through these pages, you'll meet many of my mall walking friends. They have brightened my life, and they will be at your side, encouraging you all the way as you become fitter, leaner, and, I dare say, happier.

In my enthusiasm, I built a resource as huge and all-encompassing as the mall where I walk—Mall of America in Bloomington, Minnesota. Think of *Mall Walking Madness* as a giant shopping center filled with easy, fun, practical strategies and tips on how you can use mall walking to get fit, lose pounds, and stay healthy. Anything you could possibly want to know about mall walking for total fitness and weight management is contained between these covers, starting with part I, The Mall Walker's Guide to Fitness, Weight Loss, and Fun. You'll learn everything from finding a mall that's right for you to choosing walking shoes for added comfort and support to how to navigate the food court for convenient treats that don't undo all the good of the lively steps you've taken that day. Most importantly, you'll learn about how to embrace mall walking and make it one of the most rewarding, fun parts of your life!

You may have noticed how easily I can gush about mall walking. That's because I know what it does for me and my friends—and what it can do for you. Unlike most other sports and activities, you can walk at a pace that is reasonable enough to do long term without injury and yet vigorous enough to provide an excellent workout. In order to make the most of this workout, I've developed the WalkSport Fit Forever Program in part II, which starts you off easy with mall walking and weight management goals. The first of the program's two components is the 8–Week Workout. This no–fail plan was designed as an easy, fun, and effective way to get you started with mall walking. This gentle start helps you experience success immediately and gain confidence. Each week you'll pick up the mall walking pace. After a few weeks, you'll learn a special workout that incorporates strength and flexibility exercises into your mall walking sessions.

The second component is the 8-in-8 weight loss plan, using mall walking to help you lose 8 pounds in 8 weeks. You'll make changes in your diet and nutrition, use a diary to plan meals and record weight loss, write goals and affirmations, control your cravings, think about serving size, enlist the support of partners and family, eat guilt-free at restaurants, and much more. You'll lose 8 pounds, which may seem like a modest amount, but think of it: They'll be gone *forever.* That's what the Walk-Sport Fit Forever Program does—gives you the tools and knowledge not only to lose the weight, but to keep it off for good.

My mall walking friends and I want you to walk with us for the fun and the social buzz—and for your health. The initiative to gain total fitness and manage your weight will have to come from you— truly, the next step is yours—but we're going to be right there at your side, offering advice and encouragement. So, come on, meet us at the mall!

Part I

The Mall Walker's Guide to Fitness, Weight Loss, and FUN

1

The Call of the Mall

People often ask me what inspired me to start walking at the mall. I tell them the truth—my son Peter's nosiness.

Fourteen years ago—just as I was about to embark on yet another diet—Peter lassoed me with this question:

"Mom, why do you go on diets?"

The obvious answer was to lose weight, but Peter had seen me diet before, and he knew diets didn't seem to work. What weight I had lost I'd always gained back. Standing there in the kitchen, the answer to his question was not so obvious. Why *did* I go on diets?

As an operating-room nurse, I observed the link between obesity and heart disease and understood the need to lose weight. I had seen arteries lined with plaque, flaccid hearts covered with fat, and other problems related to obesity. I knew exercising just three times a week could tone my heart and cut my risk of heart disease in half.

In the span of just a few seconds, I finally realized the futility of all my woeful deprivation diets. I turned to face my son.

"Peter," I said, "You're right. I'm finished with dieting. That is my promise to you."

My Road of Good Intentions

A dozen chocolate chip cookies and not a minute of exercise later, my body started its typical postdiet weight gain. I came face-to-face with that slip of a vow to my son. *Now* what was I going to do? Being "fat" again was simply not a healthy option, and I had just made a cross-my-heart pledge to my son to stop dieting. I decided right then to find a form of exercise I could live with—and even enjoy—for the rest of my life.

I had a rather checkered history with exercise. I used to run up and down the beautiful boulevards of my neighborhood in St. Paul, Minnesota, but I could never sustain a run for more than a few frantic blocks. Now, however, steeled by my promise to Peter and determined to prove that resolve can be a triumph of hope over experience, I set out to become a diligent runner.

My triumph was short-lived. I experienced 6 weeks of lower back pain and required several physical therapy sessions. When my doctor suggested I give up running, I secretly gave thanks.

Next I joined a high-impact aerobics class. I liked the music and dancing, and the class was fairly close to home. I bought an outfit to look the part, which I covered up with a hefty sweatshirt. Dancing to the music, I moved more or less in synch with the others. But my back gave out again.

Then, my doctor suggested walking.

"What can walking do for me?" I scoffed. "I mean, this girl likes cookies—lots of them."

I was desperate, so I decided to give walking a try. It was February—too cold for outdoor walking in Minnesota—so I joined a local health club with an indoor track. A lonely, deserted, boring track. I trudged ahead, but after 2 weeks I was close to quitting. I even was beginning to think that being fat would be . . . okay.

Just then a racewalking clinic came to my club. To my surprise, I found racewalking challenging. It required focus and technique, and it didn't hurt my back. This type of walking wasn't boring, and since I race-walked with others, I was no longer lonely. I enjoyed racewalking so much, I even competed in some national races.

Sadly, my racewalking career, too, was fleeting. A few weeks after a race, my gym went bankrupt and shut its doors for good. But by a stroke of serendipity, about the same time, Mall of America opened. I didn't see the mall as a fantastic shopping center in Bloomington, Minnesota. I saw Mall of America as a new, state-of-the-art walking track that I could use—for free.

I started walking at Mall of America the minute its doors were open. And ten years later, it's still my favorite place to walk. While running and aerobics were not for me, mall walking made me a lifetime exerciser. It helps me keep my weight down and my spirits up. Just by walking each day, I have kept 15 pounds off, gained muscle, dropped a full dress size, and eat the foods I want (in moderation, of course). And yes, I have kept my promise to my son: I have never gone on another diet.

The Mall Walking Movement

While my life was revolutionized by mall walking, my story is not unusual. In fact, mall walking is almost 50 years old, having begun just shortly after the first mall opened its doors.

The Southdale Shopping Center, the first totally enclosed mall in the United States, opened in Edina, Minnesota, in 1956. Minneapolis doctors advised patients recovering from heart attacks to exercise at Southdale, where they would not have to risk walking on snow and ice. This eventually led to an organized mall walking community. By the 1980s, a nationwide boom in mall construction coincided with a nationwide concern about overweight Americans. Often with the support of local medical communities, mall walking took off.

Today, the path to mall walking has become well-worn by the nearly 2.5 million people who walk in the nation's 1,800 malls. Some of these folks have never considered themselves exercisers but are drawn to mall walking by a friend, the safety of the mall, the controlled climate, the level floors, or the shops. Others, like me, come limping into the mall, all banged up. Many of them were runners, bikers, swimmers, or aerobic dancers searching for fitness. They found "the burn" but, too often, were also burned by injuries. Finally, when they were too sore—or too bored—they tried mall walking.

It makes no difference to me how people come to mall walking. I just love to see them walking and to be with them as they do. What a joy it is when folks who've been indifferent to or discouraged by exercise in the past take those first few steps toward a healthier lifestyle. I love to see them smile, because they know mall walking is easy, fun, and perfect for them.

That's why I started WalkSport America—I wanted to be a part of that exciting transformation. When I do my classes and workshops on walking, I draw from my nursing background, my extensive study of walking, and my training in exercise physiology to show people how to make mall walking work for them. After I speak, I then teach "on the fly," casting seeds of information and inspiration. At one speaking engagement, I was introduced as a modern-day, mall walking Joanie Appleseed.

Most of all, I love to walk with people. As I walk with these friendly folks, I learn how people make mall walking work as a workout and, sometimes, as a powerful agent of change.

How Mall Walking Can Change You

You may have read a great deal about weight management in books and magazines, but the reality is, shedding pounds doesn't have to be that complex. Taking that first simple step at the mall can lead to a whole new way to look at weight loss and, possibly, a whole new start to your life.

Mall walking is an activity that gives everyone a chance to succeed. Once you start, you realize how doable it is and you just *know* you can do the exercise you need for weight management. When I tried other forms of exercise, I always worried that boredom or injury would keep me from my workouts. Not so with mall walking. I know many people like me, who have tried and failed repeatedly to lose weight. Then we tried mall walking and succeeded!

Mall walking is an all-embracing exercise. We don't turn away anyone who is not big, slim, fast, young, or old enough. What the Statue of Liberty is to immigrants, malls are to all the "huddled masses" of exercisers. The barriers that keep people from sticking with other forms of exercise—weather, expense, boredom, and injuries—are all but absent with mall walking. I like being part of such a welcoming, life-long activity.

Malls Are Ideal for Exercise

A few years ago, a delightful reporter for a Japanese radio station interviewed me, asking questions about mall walking and WalkSport. She was very impressed by the number of walkers at Mall of America, the guest speakers at our monthly meetings, and the camaraderie at our occasional breakfast meetings.

During the interview, I stepped back and tried to see the mall and this mall walking phenomenon through the reporter's eyes. Sometimes I forget just how exciting and even beautiful malls can be. When I step inside a mall, I often feel a buzz, a marketplace mania. (I know I get a gleam in my eye when I'm packing plastic.) But rather than see the green plants and bright flowers as a backdrop simply for shopping, we mall people truly appreciate them—especially in the dead of winter. We love the smells that remind us of the state fair—the cinnamon buns, the coffee, the caramel corn. We enjoy the decorated atriums, especially at the holidays, and we're grateful for the entertainment—the singers, Santas, and school bands. Some malls even have rides and attractions to watch. At Mall of America, Camp Snoopy features the Log Chute, Mystery Mine Ride, the Mighty Axe, Ghost Blasters, and the Screaming Yellow Eagle.

And, of course, there are the shops themselves. We become intimately acquainted with all the offers lurking in the corners of the mall, and we study the campaigns each merchant uses to lure people into his store. With all the flirting mannequins, signs with BOLDFACE and exclamation points!!!! and dazzling displays, it's hard to get bored at a mall.

I reflected on all this while I talked with the Japanese reporter, wondering if she shared my thinking. When they are at their best, malls give Americans a place to meet and celebrate the choice and freedom in our

Beth Changed One "Silly" Thing

Four years ago, Beth weighed 240 pounds. She was coming out of a "disastrous marriage," as she puts it, and living a life that included making ends meet with food stamps. She worked in a mall in Charlotte, North Carolina, and one day some of her office mates asked if she would join them for a walk in the mall. Even though Beth says in the past she used "every excuse in the book" for not exercising, this time she said "yes." She was stressed, and she thought the companionship would do her good.

"I made it halfway around the mall, and I thought I needed a ventilator," Beth recalls. "I couldn't even walk four steps without gasping. My whole goal was to get back to the office."

Beth's friends kept asking her to walk, and for the first 2 weeks she reluctantly kept saying "yes," partly because she describes herself as such a "pleaser" that she just couldn't say "no." Then after the second week she noticed she was . . . well, feeling better.

"The mall walking had a calming influence," she says. "I did not lose weight, but I felt less stressed, like I was getting healthier, gaining control of my life."

Beth liked the walking but not the noontime crowds. In the third week she started to come to work early to walk the mall. "I didn't want anyone to see

economy. Malls are our present-day urban community, replacing town squares and sidewalks where people used to congregate and walk around their neighborhood. Considering the millions of Americans who are looking for interesting ways to be active, the mall seems like the perfect place to find community and exercise under one roof.

The reporter interrupted my musings by pointing out an obvious irony—people have to *drive* in order to *walk* at the mall. She laughed in a my fat legs," she says. "I was very self-conscious. I didn't want people to think that I was divorced and now trying to 'fix myself up' with walking. So I walked 30 to 45 minutes in the morning, feeling safe from the humiliation."

Beth didn't go on a diet but started eating low-fat meals. She watched her fat intake and continued walking in the mornings and sometimes in the evenings as well. But she hadn't lost a pound. "Then, all of a sudden, at the end of 2 months, my body got the message and the weight just started coming off," Beth says. From Labor Day to Thanksgiving that year, she lost 45 pounds. By the next spring, she lost a total of 100.

Four years later, Beth is in a relationship again and happy to have kept most of the weight off. When a move to a different house meant more time commuting and less time walking, she regained 15 pounds. But she knows what to do to lose the weight again. "It does not always have to do with dieting," she says. "The only way for me is to walk my way back to health. As long as I can walk, I don't have to worry about it."

Beth's message to us? Never underestimate the power of taking that first step toward change. "I just changed one thing—I started walking—and it has had that much impact," she says. "People ask me how I did it. I tell them, and then they ask again: How did I *really* do it? I tell them to just go for a walk every day. Just changing that one 'silly' thing was so simple, but it empowered me to make other changes in my life and then others still."

"gotcha" sort of way, and I had to laugh, too. After all, she had me there! But her pointing out mall walking's one disadvantage only helped to further underscore the list of advantages mall walking had over most other forms of activity.

- **Mall walking is for everyone.** It can be done by exercise neophytes and fitness fanatics alike.

- **Mall walking is inexpensive, requiring just walking shoes.** Malls are the cheapest health clubs in town!

- **Mall walking can be done in any weather.** When the weather outside is frightful, inside it's so delightful—about 70 degrees. In the mall's controlled climate, it is never too hot, cold, windy, rainy, snowy, buggy, or muggy.

- **Mall walking offers safety.** No need to worry about slippery, cracked, or uneven surfaces; dogs nipping at your heels; or muggers lurking by the escalators. You will never be run over by bicyclists, rollerbladers, or skateboarders. It's highly unlikely that bees or other insects will bother you, or that you will be overwhelmed by allergens, noise, or air pollution. If you do have some sort of accident or health problem, people in malls will offer a helping hand. Malls offer security guards, well-lit spaces, and access to telephones. Many malls have health clinics as well. Bottom line, while you're in the mall, chances are you're safe.

- **Mall walking offers convenience.** Malls are usually near main roads and easy to find. Once there, you can stow stuff not needed for your workout in lockers. Malls often provide strollers, if you need one for your child.

- **Malls provide free parking.** No hassle and lost time finding a parking spot. No feeding meters and then rushing through workouts to beat the meter. Just park, lose yourself in your workout, and then relax afterward.

- **Malls are clean.** Mall walking erases the need to stare at your feet while you walk. I guarantee you, no matter where you step, there'll be no dog or goose doo-doo to dance around.

- **Malls have restrooms.** While mall walking, you don't have to answer nature's call behind a bush.

- **Malls have water fountains and benches.** You can stay well-hydrated without lugging water bottles or strapping on camel packs. Benches are good for rest stops, which are important for beginners who lack stamina. They're also useful for stretching and upper body exercises such as dips and pushups. We'll talk about these special exercises in part II.

● **Oh, did I mention the shopping?**

Finding a Walker-Friendly Mall

You've seen how mall walking stands head and shoulders above other exercise in terms of convenience, safety, and entertainment value. Now, it's a matter of getting you to the mall to start walking. So, just pick any mall and start walking, right?

Not exactly. While most malls welcome mall walkers, a few don't. You may have read about Evergreen Plaza, a mall in the Chicago suburb of Evergreen Park. One February, management proclaimed that the mall would no longer be available to walkers. The management complained that the mall walkers muddied freshly buffed floors, hogged prime parking spots, demanded free Christmas gifts, and were not exactly loose with their money. They also claimed that opening the mall to before-business-hours walkers presented security and liability concerns.

Well, this just plain outraged the Evergreen mall walking community. Some of them had exercised there for 20 years. Walkers wrote letters to the 125 mall merchants, telling them they would take their business elsewhere because of this mall walking ban. The Chicago news media hopped all over this story, and Evergreen Plaza's smart competitors seized the opportunity and began stealing its shoppers. Other malls distributed handouts in and around Evergreen Plaza, inviting mall walkers to their malls. One mall even offered free refreshments and meditation classes. Stunned and burned by the bad publicity and patron poaching, Evergreen Plaza management quickly raised the white flag. One week after the ban-the-walkers proclamation, the mall welcomed mall walkers once again. Some miffed mall walkers defected, but, ironically, the publicity attracted a huge crop of rookie mall walkers to the Plaza. One report said the number of registered mall walkers at Evergreen more than doubled, to more than 1,200.

The following year, I was quoted in a front page *New York Times* article about the supposed "strain" that can sometimes exist between mall managers and mall walkers. To my surprise, even David Letterman did a short routine on his *Late Show* about this mall walking issue, which was taking on the appearance of a controversy.

I assure you, there is no controversy.

Yes, mall walkers occasionally forget they are mall guests, and a few mall walkers have been known to take advantage of a mall's generosity. And yes, sometimes malls forget what a significant financial contribution their walkers make. For the most part, though, it is a mutually supportive and satisfying relationship, especially when mall walkers follow the advice below about how to pick the best mall for them and how to work with the management to ensure that there are no conflicts.

First, pick three or four malls close to your home. Then, visit each of them, armed with these questions.

- Do the doors open early for mall walkers? Look for a mall that will be open to mall walkers when you prefer to walk.

- Which doors open earliest? Don't waste time wandering around the outside of the mall searching for an open door when you go to walk.

- Does the mall feel uplifting? You should like the lighting, cleanliness, decorations, smells, sights, and types of stores in the mall.

- What are the mall's features and size? Stairs add variety to your workout, and escalators are great when you are pooped out after a good walk. Straight or rectangular malls are great for doing laps. Many walkers prefer malls with two or more floors to add interest to their walks. Some walkers want malls big enough so they can rack up many miles in each workout. If the mall management can't tell you how big the mall is, you can determine its size with a pedometer or a measuring wheel.

- Is there a formal walking program already in place at the mall? If so, ask about benefits of the program and for registration information. Also inquire about methods used to log your walking time or distance, and if the program offers awards. Ask other walkers at that mall if they like the program. Also ask them if merchants are friendly to mall walkers. If the mall doesn't have a formal walking program, consider starting one yourself.

- Is there a fee to join? Avoid going for the cheapest program in town. Often, you get what you pay for. Generally, mall walking programs run from free to $15, as a one-time fee.

- Is there a check-in-check-out system? Logging your miles and time can be an effective motivational tool.

- Are you required to wear identification or sign an injury waiver form? These measures protect the malls.

- Is there a place to put coats and bags? The availability of lockers may seem like a small matter, but it isn't. It's best to walk in workout clothes, *sans* heavy coat. Leaving your coat on a bench is risky and sometimes irksome to mall managers, who want a tidy look to their malls. During the winter, leaving your coat in the car can be unhealthy. Racing in is no problem, but coming out tired and sweaty, when it's 10 degrees below zero is definitely not health-enhancing.

Once you get the answers to these questions and others that may be important to you, it will become clear which mall is best for you.

The Only Equipment You'll Need: Quality Shoes

Now that you know where you're going to mall walk, you should take a good hard look at the only gear that you'll need: a pair of quality walking shoes.

Is it technically possible to mall walk in any shoes? Sure. Should you? No! Good shoes equal happy feet, backs, and joints. Many mall walkers don't think about their walking shoes, however, and they keep on trucking with worn-out shoes. Maybe we suffer from shoe loyalty—we wear our favorite shoes year after year, even though the support has been squished out of them. If you're that loyal, use them to mow the lawn. They won't support you on the hard surfaces of the mall, and they can make you more susceptible to injury.

When I first looked into walking shoes, I remember asking, "What's the deal? I have walked for years, so why do I need specialty shoes?" I confess that the stubborn little girl in me resisted buying a "walking" shoe. I had good-looking aerobic shoes, thank you, and I wasn't about to change. After 3 weeks of determined walking, though, my heel started to get a painful ridge on it. Then it hit me: Maybe there was something to this walking shoe thing. Since then, I've learned a podiatrists' rule of thumb: If you do an activity two or three times a week, buy the activity-specific shoe. That definitely meant I needed walking shoes.

I went to a few shoe shops and tried on a variety of shoes, and boy, was I in for a shock. For the first time in my life, I could feel the support under the arches of my feet. I remember saying to the salesperson: "Is it really supposed to feel like that?" So began my walking shoe education, which has continued with the help of podiatrists and shoe technicians.

Buying the Best Walking Shoes for You

Maybe one reason we avoid shopping for shoes is that choosing from all the options available can be overwhelming. First, not all feet are alike. Ask a podiatrist to explain pronating feet, supinating feet, high-arched feet, flat feet, or the different types of lasts (basic forms around which shoes are built) that shoe companies manufacture, and the answers will numb your mind.

Second, not all shoes are alike, even if, at first blush, they appear fine for mall walking. Trying to differentiate between the various types of athletic shoes can be bewildering to beginners attempting to find the most appropriate shoes. To that end, I offer you this primer.

Buy early and buy often. All too often, we decide we don't need new shoes because of the expense or because the shoes still look good, but podiatrists advise changing walking shoes after 400 to 500 miles of use, or in 6 to 9 months. Even if the outside looks good, if you've had your shoes for a while, the midsole—the less visible but most critical, shock-absorbing part of the shoe that usually wears out first—is probably shot. In that case, you are waiting for pain—not miles or months—to prompt the change.

The best strategy to ensure that you replace them on time is to write the date of purchase and the projected change date in permanent marker on the tongue or sole of your shoes, so you can see this date each time you lace up. When the change date comes, remember, no excuses!

Get expert help. Once you are convinced that walking shoes are for you, go to a store staffed with salespeople who are thoroughly trained in fitting shoes. Even if you think you know your shoe size, get both of your feet measured. Some people have different-sized feet and need different-sized shoes. Also, your feet can grow and change in your adult years. Have your feet measured late in the afternoon when they are slightly swollen. Wear the socks that you use for walking.

Invest in the good stuff. With walking shoes, you get what you pay for, so don't bother with the cheapies that feel good today and wear out tomorrow. Expect to spend $60 or more for good shoes, which have the lightness, technology, and construction features athletes demand.

Okay, let's say you are in the store and have reached the trying-on stage. Shopping works best when you know the function of each shoe part. So here's a quick look at shoe parts.

- **Upper:** Leather or leather-synthetic mesh material that makes up most of the outer shoe. Should be breathable. Uppers often have a reinforced toebox for protection.

- **Outsole:** Bottom of the sole, where the rubber (or polyurethane) meets the road. Grooves typically are shallow to prevent tripping.

- **Midsole:** Between the outsole and the upper, this is the all-important cushioning part of the shoe. Made of EVA (ethyl vinyl acetate) or polyurethane, the midsole may contain air or gel pads.

- **Insole:** This padded and removable part is where your foot touches the shoe. Replacing insoles can make the shoes feel new.

- **Toebox:** Front area of the shoe that must be roomy and flexible enough to allow toes and forefeet the space to spread and push off.

- **Heel counter:** Stiff cup needed for rearfoot stability.

Now that you've got the lingo down, you can use it to evaluate your favorites for the three features of good walking shoes.

1. **Forefoot flexibility.** Pick up the shoe and flex the forefoot area. Compare shoes, looking for the difference in stiffness. Notice that the soles curve up at heel and toe. This allows your foot to "roll" better through each step.

2. **Modest heel cushioning.** Walking shoes have less heel cushioning than running shoes because there is less downward force on the heel area with each walking step. If you are heavy or have joint pain, you may want to use a running shoe because of this extra cushioning. However, it's better for most walkers to avoid shoes with super-cushioned heels, which can cause a forefoot-to-floor slapping motion that can lead to sore shins.

3. **Snug heel counters.** This provides the heel constant support during the entire heel-to-toe motion of each step. A flimsy or loose-fitting heel counter makes for an uncomfortable walk and is a setup for potential injuries. Some heel counters will fit better than others, so compare different brands and styles.

As you try on different shoes, keep in mind that a good fit leaves you with ½ inch of toe room. Also, the shoes should feel good right away; you should not have to break them in. Take your shoes for a spin in the store and in the mall. Walk briskly, as you would during a workout.

Gone are the days when you did just about any sport or physical activity in something called "sneakers." To a certain degree, this is the result of marketers and shoe manufacturers first creating, then filling, a need. But consumers must also take some credit. Walking shoes are here to stay because of your increasing interest in caring for your health, including your feet. Taking care of your feet means reducing the risk of injuries in the ankles, legs, knees, hips, back, and body parts on up the line.

One more point about walking shoes: The future of these shoes is exciting. Boasting gadgets galore, the future's walking shoes will come equipped with pedometers, calorie counters, heart rate monitors, computer chips, magnets, and—get this—speakers that help you train and cheer you on. Futurists, the not-too-distant kind, say there will be shoes that sense the distribution of pressure on your foot and automatically adjust the cushioning as you walk. (For gadgets available in the here-and-now, see "Mall Walkers' Top 10 Toys" on page 22, and see "Resources for Walkers" on page 219 for buying information.)

Mall Walking Etiquette

You're set for shoes, and you've narrowed down your search to the perfect mall for you. No doubt your search gave you a heightened appreciation of what wonderful places malls can be, especially the one you've selected as "your" mall. Not only does your mall have a pleasant atmosphere and cooperative management, it will also be the place where you get great workouts for years to come. As part of your appreciation for your mall, try to make every effort to get along with management, merchants, and shoppers. To that end, here are some mall walking etiquette guidelines.

Remember, this is a *shopping* mall. The mall is in the business of leasing space—for money. If mall owners didn't get revenue from store leases, there'd be no reason to build this enclosed space that so wonderfully accommodates us mall walkers. Management's purpose is to drive shoppers to their stores. They draw good tenants by demonstrating that their mall is good for sales. Therefore, if you really want to make mall managers happy to have walkers, spend your money at the mall. And when you do, let merchants know you are a mall walker.

Many merchants understand that walkers spend money at their mall, and yet some say, "Oh, those walkers are only here for the free stuff—they don't spend anything." In some cases, they are right, but for the most part, mall walkers bring business to the mall. In my WalkSport travels, I

(continued on page 24)

Mall Walkers' Top 10 Toys

With all the time you'll spend window-shopping and chatting, chances are you'll never have need of distraction. Still, sometimes toys can make a good thing even better. Check out these favorite gadgets of mall walkers everywhere.

1. Step counter. This device, smaller than a pager, is worn at the waist. It counts your steps every time your body makes enough impact to trigger the counting mechanism. The American College of Sports Medicine and the Centers for Disease Control and Prevention recommend that Americans walk about 10,000 steps per day, but most Americans only take 2,000 to 4,000. You can usually get to 10,000 by making a 30- to 40-minute walk part of each day.

I wear a step counter every day. If I see that I've only taken 7,000 steps by dinner, I'll get up and tap dance, climb the stairs, walk up and down the hallway a few more times—anything that gets me to that magic 10,000-step mark.

2. CD and/or tape player. Listen to your favorite music, walking to the beat of up-tempo songs. Check out books on tape from a library. Try a mystery or suspense novel that you can't "put down," and let yourself listen to it only when you are walking. Try self-improvement tapes, or learn a language on tape or CD. Promise yourself that once you learn conversational Italian, you'll reward yourself with a trip to Rome.

3. AM/FM radio. Some pocket-size radios have TV—and weather channel—sound options. Don't *wait* to walk because you might miss your favorite soap or news show. Listen to it *while* you walk.

4. Heart rate monitor. This device goes around your chest, under your clothing. It detects your pulse, which you read on a wristwatch display. A monitor helps you raise your heart rate to get a good workout, but it prevents you from pushing too hard and putting yourself at risk. If you are like me, you might find yourself dilly-dallying when you start talking while walking. A heart rate monitor reminds you to stay on task.

5. Upper-body workout belt. This device, called the PowerBelt, has two handles attached to cords that connect to a pulley system within the belt. As you walk, you grab the handles and pump your arms. This movement exercises your arms, shoulders, and chest at the same time that your legs are getting a workout. According to the manufacturer's research, using this belt can help you burn up to 71 percent more calories than regular walking.

6. Walking poles. Like ski poles with rubber tips, these are nice for mall walking and hiking outside. They provide extra stability, and by distributing some of your weight to the poles, you can put less pressure on achy knees. Finally, poles can give your upper body a workout if you push off with them as if you are cross-country skiing.

7. Hand weights. These are easy to pack in a bag before going to the mall. Keep the weights light (no more than 1.5 pounds each), and use them to build your upper body while walking. I am surprised at how well hand weights tone my muscles and maximize my workout time.

8. Tally counter. If you can't seem to use your fingers, or memory, to keep track of how many laps you've done, this gadget's for you. Carry a tally counter in the palm of your hand and click it once for each lap.

9. Tape recorder. I have heard it said that walking oils the gears of the mind. So true. When I walk, I churn up many good ideas. Sometimes I bring a micro cassette recorder on my walks to record these ideas. You can use the recorder to dictate letters and record perishable thoughts.

10. Calorie counter. Simply clip this beeper-size counter to your waist, and it records your daily caloric expenditure. Seeing the number of calories I burn always motivates me to burn more!

One fancy model, the Fit Sense FS1, has many of the features of a treadmill. A foot pod (about the size of half a hard boiled egg) attaches to your shoelaces, containing software that computes your speed, distance, and calories burned. This data is displayed on a wristwatch. As an option, you can purchase the FS1 with a heart rate monitor and an FS net link, which transfers all your data to your computer. Now, that's what I call a toy!

always ask groups of walkers about their spending habits at malls, and almost all say they are great spenders. When I ask this question, a few mall walkers usually point at new shirts worn by their buddies, who had told their spouses about a good sale, who'd in turn told their friends, and *their* friends, and so on and so on. Those are living examples of word-of-mouth advertising, something merchants tell me is the best kind.

Park in areas designated for mall walkers. Some malls frown upon walkers taking the good parking spots. Often we take the good spots unintentionally, because we are so accustomed to seeking out the most convenient parking place wherever we go. But don't forget—you're going to the mall to exercise, so why not let it begin by parking where the management wants and walking a little farther?

Even when management makes no parking designations for mall walkers, it's still a good idea to park a few rows back from the door or on the top level of multilevel parking. However, if you walk and then shop, feel free to park near the door so you can easily haul your purchases to the car.

Take time to thank merchants. Certainly when you make a purchase and even when you don't, go out of your way to thank merchants for allowing you to walk at the mall. Get to know them, and give them a smile and a greeting from time to time. When you bring friends and relatives to shop, eat, or play at the mall, let merchants know mall walkers bring merchants business.

When merchants want help, give it to them. Sometimes merchants look for a way to get their message out to the mall walking community. Making an effort to say "yes" to their requests can create a lot of good will. A few merchants have asked mall walkers to provide temporary help, such as with inventory. Again, think about saying "yes."

Don't take freebies for granted. I was once at a mall and Ruby Tuesday, a restaurant, set out free coffee for walkers before their normal business hours. Some grateful walkers took up a collection to pay for Styrofoam cups, thus keeping costs down for the Ruby Tuesday people. These gestures of appreciation go a long way toward building and maintaining good will. Unfortunately, some thoughtless people took the coffee carafes up to another level where there were tables in a court-yard—and started demanding refills of the coffee. The freebie coffee promptly ended.

Smile and greet those you meet on your walk. By smiling, you're doing your small but important part to make the mall a pleasant place to be. A few years ago, a producer for the Discovery Channel was in the Twin Cities filming a special on malls, covering everything from the building of the first mall to how malls have evolved into glitzy enter-tainment centers. After a few days of filming at Mall of America and in-terviewing mall walkers, he said he understood why there is such an uplifting spirit at this mall: The mall walkers are so friendly and look so happy.

I am not saying you should constantly wear a smile plastered to your face as you walk the mall—that would wear you out. Just smile once in a while, and see what happens. Over the years, I have made it a habit to smile at people wherever I walk. I just smile as I pass people, and more than once I have been told how nice it was to see a bright smile.

Yield to everyone. Again, this is a shopping destination above all, so groups of shoppers should be able to do their thing without having you weave in and out of them as you walk. I certainly have been guilty of this—during brisk walks with friends, it's easy to get into the workout, start talking, and then not pay attention to traffic. But I have learned that whipping around people can startle, annoy, or even hurt them, never mind what can happen when you crash into them. Be cautious around slower walkers and shoppers.

Don't be a wall hugger. One of the less endearing quirks of some mall walkers is their determination to walk along the wall of the mall and not to yield to anyone. They want to cover the most mileage they can in their walk, and they figure they can do so by staying along the wall where the circumference of their loop is the largest. An unsuspecting shopper who also happens to be walking the wall may find himself suddenly in-volved in a game of "chicken." The mall walker hangs in there and forces the shopper to go around. This is a no-no. Avoid silly games of chicken, and let shoppers have their walls.

Don't walk in a broad bunch. More than three walkers side by side really clogs up hallways. This is especially true of parents pushing strollers. You don't want to be an intimidating "flying wedge" of walkers bulldozing through throngs of shoppers, so walk three abreast at the most.

Help bewildered shoppers. Introduce yourself as a mall walker and ask if the person needs help locating a store. It's all part of making the mall a pleasant place to be.

Be the eyes and ears of the mall. Report icky bathrooms, suspicious characters, or foul play. Do it in the spirit of a friendly suggestion; don't be a pest. Remember, you want the mall management to know that you are on their side.

How to Start a Mall Walking Club

Once you start walking at a mall, you will probably start making friends with other mall walkers. One friend leads to another and then another, and pretty soon you have a group with a common bond. If your mall doesn't have a formal mall walking club, you may decide to start one. How can you do this?

First, call customer service at the mall. Ask the kinds of questions we covered in the section on how to find a walker-friendly mall. The general idea is to find out if the mall is willing to sanction a mall walking club, provide a meeting space, permit refreshments, and help promote club activities. Their answers will give you a sense of management's willingness to welcome you and work with you.

Of course, I would love it if you contacted me at WalkSport America (651-291-7138 and www.walksport.com). I can guide you through the process of developing a mall walking club. (I'll also make every effort to come to your mall for a kick-off party!) WalkSport offers members a newsletter and health seminars. We also provide clubs with an exclusive electronic card reader that members use to record their walking times and tally calories burned while walking. A report of each member's status is sent monthly to the mall and is also available on our Web site. All of our WalkSport malls are part of the same system, so you can use your card and stay on track even when you are traveling. We ship merchandise awards to members as they reach goals, and we have all sorts of free gifts, special drawings, promotions, and discounts.

Whether you set up your own club or join the WalkSport family, the important thing is that you and your friends are coming together with a shared commitment to mall walking and good health. As I have said before, this is a kinder and gentler exercise that excludes almost no one; you're in if you can get to the mall and walk. And once you are in, you can start stepping and grinning.

Discovering Your Own Mall Walking Community

In 1997, I received a call from Dr. Thomas Kottke, a cardiologist at the Mayo Clinic in Rochester, Minnesota. "I heard about the mall walking program you have at Mall of America," he said. "I want you to start the same thing down here in Rochester." He added that he liked how the program created a "community of health."

Dr. Kottke shared stories about his cardiology patients. He always told them to avoid fatty foods and to exercise every day. Sure, they replied, no problem. Then he watched them walk out of his office into a community of people gorging on fast food and sitting for hours in front of computer screens and television sets.

"The community doesn't act healthfully," Dr. Kottke said, "so how can I expect my patients to change?"

Mall walking programs solve this problem by creating positive peer pressure. Through these programs, we see people taking good care of themselves in a highly public place. Mall walkers demonstrate healthful habits for the community at large.

When you step into the mall walking community, you walk with people who are concerned about the health and well-being of themselves and other mall walkers. Mary Jaroz, who does the blood pressure checks at the Chicago Ridge Mall, tells me that if a mall walker gets sick or has surgery, the word spreads; other walkers send get-well cards and visit the hospital. Mall walking no-shows get a concerned call. If one mall walker hears of a mall event or sale, the news spreads like wildfire. Roberta Cygan, in customer service at that same mall, says walkers exchange plants and bulbs at the WalkSport card reader, which becomes a "water cooler," of sorts, for mall walkers. She says after their regular walks, groups of 10 to 20 mall walkers chat over coffee, and occasionally a mall walking romance blooms.

These kinds of personal touches happen in most mall walking communities. People get to know each other as they walk together, and it is only natural that they start caring for one another. Here at Mall of America, walkers gather Tuesday mornings in the food court. They buy coffee at Burger King, and someone brings a cake to celebrate birthdays. People in the program are surprised and thrilled to find a card, with lots of signatures, in the mailbox on their birthdays.

I think of Stewart, who lost 114 pounds mall walking. "It's because of your smiling faces and ongoing encouragement," he says to his mall walking friends, "that I have continued to come and walk. It is also because when I don't come for a day or two, you say, 'Hey, where ya been?'"

One woman wrote me a note saying that after her husband died, mall walking got her out of bed each day. "Without other people to share my life with, I don't know what I would have done," she said.

I hear story after story of how mall walkers pull each other along. Don, a former swimmer and runner, told me he had Parkinson's disease. "My doctor said it would be best to keep as healthy and fit as possible to hold off symptoms. So I walk," he said. "My medication works better when I walk. I feel antsy when I don't. I'm in good shape, I can eat anything, plus I talk with other mall walkers. And because I'm in this walking club, I get 10 percent off whatever I buy at the mall!"

As we move on to the remaining chapters of the book, I hope you will make a promise to yourself to use mall walking to reach your fitness and weight management goals. Remember, mall walking brings a community of friends who share your goals—and when it comes to sticking it out for the long haul, friends are your bread for the journey.

Make the Rounds, Lose the Pounds: The Mall Walker's Weight Loss Tool Kit

Remember *Feel the burn?*

During the 1980s and early 1990s, this was our fitness mantra. For something that was supposed to make us healthier, exercise sure sounded painful! Still, we clung to the delusion that physical activity had to hurt. When it ached, chafed, or cramped, we'd push ourselves on, gritting our teeth and saying, "No pain, no gain!"

I, for one, was a huge proponent of this philosophy. Remember when I told you about my doctor's suggestion that I try walking? I scoffed—I was a runner and an aerobic dancer! Okay, a frequently injured, pained runner and dancer, but what could walking possibly do for me?

The truth is, I was responding out of ignorance about walking. I was like more than a few fitness snobs who turned up their noses at low-impact activities, especially mall walking. Too easy, we said, dismissively. Not enough intensity. *Intensity* was the key sensation that drove me to do those fast-paced activities. (I even did rock climbing for a while.) I looked at walking as a last resort, what you did when you were unable to do anything else or until you could get up the speed to get out there and go, go, go.

Very quickly, we go-go girls and guys were gone from the fitness scene, 6 months (or sometimes 6 days) after beginning whatever the "in" intense activity of the day was. Those trendy sports were just too much for many of us. Sadly, many who gave up on exercise because of burnout

MALL WALKING MAVEN

Duane Walked Away from Pain

Ask my friend Duane what he gets from mall walking and he says, "Walking is therapeutic, good for the mind." Every day, Duane begins his morning with a 2-hour walk around the mall, from 7 to 9 A.M. He's been doing this since 1995, one year after his wife's suicide.

Duane shudders to think of life without mall walking. After Marie's death, he gained 15 pounds, had trouble sleeping, and took excessive amounts of Anacin a week for chronic hip pain. "I could hardly get up from a chair," he says. The hip pain dated back to an accident when he was 10. He'd been hit by a car and seriously injured. "Doctors told me I would never walk again."

Well, Duane does walk—at a clip few can match. He wears a heart rate monitor and tears around the mall, keeping his heart rate steady at 120 beats a minute—"the high end of aerobic," as he puts it. As Duane whizzes by other walkers, it's hard to imagine him not walking. His hip seems fine (he takes just four Anacin per day) and his weight is down. "I don't diet at all," he says. "I eat well and get into all the ice creams."

When I see him zooming around the mall, I wonder at the change in Duane since his wife died. His spirits are way up, and how much of that relates to walking is anyone's guess. But when I look at how far he's come, I think Duane is onto something when he says, "I'm not going to stop walking."

or injuries joined those who'd never been among the fitness faithful anyway. The net result was a lot of people sitting on their bottoms.

This situation troubled public health officials. In the early 1990s, the American College of Sports Medicine (ACSM) announced that only 22 percent of adults engaged in leisure-time exercise at levels recommended for health benefits—a surprisingly small number considering all the cheering about exercise that had been going on in America since the 1970s. I attribute this directly to the prevailing all-or-nothing notions about exercise and intensity—many of us were just choosing nothing.

Thankfully, ACSM and other fitness groups saw what was going on, and they lowered their sights a bit. Whereas the ACSM used to tell people to exercise for 20 to 60 minutes 3 to 5 days a week at a fairly high intensity, in 1993, they changed that recommendation to 30 minutes of any moderately intense activity most days of the week. This more moderate approach was intended to woo the exercise wannabes and dropouts back into the fitness fold—and it worked, to a degree. The fitness industry came around to embrace walking, and then later mall walking, as its darling. What we mall walkers know, the experts finally learned: Walking is simple, effective, convenient, and inclusive.

Walking, the Fountain of Health

In 1956, in the Southdale Shopping Center in Edina, Minnesota, a modest Scandinavian named Ole laced up his shoes and took the very first mall walk.

Ole is still walking today, although he's very modest about his status. "I'm not sure I was the first mall walker at Southdale—somebody may have tried it before me—but I'm pretty sure that I'm the one who's been walking here the longest," Ole says. "I walk because my doctor tells me I have to. I've got diabetes and, because of it, bad circulation."

About the same time Ole was discovering the link between exercise and his own improved health, Dr. Jeremy Morris observed that heart disease death rates were lower in London bus conductors than in the bus drivers. Why? He noticed that the conductors, who climbed up the stairs to collect fares in the double-decker buses, lived longer than the drivers, who spent most of their days sitting and driving. This study was instrumental in forming the official exercise hypothesis, which states that physical activity may protect against heart disease.

Over the years, many studies have supported this exercise hypothesis, even others done in the working world. One study showed that long-shoremen who unloaded ships were less likely to die of heart disease than the clerks and foremen who did no unloading. Another found that railroad section hands lived longer than their bosses and other railroad workers in sedentary jobs.

Since these studies first appeared some 40 years ago, thousands more have revealed the many health benefits of exercise. We now know that exercise, and certainly mall walking, can lead to:

Better breathing. As your body adapts to walking, your circulation improves and your lungs become more efficient at providing the extra oxygen the body needs for physical activity. You remember John the Jokester, the Robin Williams of mall walking, from this book's introduction? If he didn't have good breathing because of mall walking, he would not be able to go nonstop with his one-liners as he walks.

A stronger heart. An important training effect of mall walking is that the heart becomes more efficient, pumping out more blood per beat and beating fewer times per minute. You get more energy with less wear and tear on your body.

Lower blood pressure. Several studies concluded that activities like brisk walking or running can cause a 10 point average reduction in both the systolic and diastolic measures (the upper and lower numbers) in the resting blood pressures of people with hypertension. Beth, from chapter 1, had a blood pressure around 150/90 when she started mall walking. Exercise dropped it to 120/65.

Lower cholesterol. Exercise training studies suggest that about 10 miles a week, or 2½ hours, of brisk walking reduces cholesterol levels, which is no sweat for most regular mall walkers.

Stronger immunity. Taking full advantage of the maxim, "less is more," mall walking is an excellent example of the kind of moderate exercise that can boost immunity. In contrast, research shows that exercise that is too strenuous and intense can actually weaken the immune system.

Increased muscular strength, endurance, flexibility, and balance. These benefits are especially important as we age. While many older beginners can be unsteady on their feet at first, mall walking increases their strength, endurance, and balance, which helps them avoid dangerous falls.

Stronger bones. When muscles move, they tug at the bones that are attached to them. This tugging stimulates bone growth, which keeps bones dense, firm, and healthy, helping fight osteoporosis. Many women come to mall walking because of their concerns about this debilitating bone disease, but everyone needs to work on keeping their bones hardy and strong.

Better bowels. Exercise helps stimulate muscle movement of the large intestine, called peristalsis. This helps with regularity. One study showed 17 percent of people who did hardly any exercise had trouble with constipation compared with only 9 percent of highly active people.

Better sleep. Working out enhances sleep by burning off tensions and allowing body and mind to unwind—and who among us couldn't use a better night's rest? A study of Army recruits in basic training found that their new exercise program decreased the time it took to fall asleep, increased their time spent in deep sleep, and boosted their total sleep time per night.

Less depression. I saved this benefit for last, because I wanted to talk about it in detail. Depression can affect all areas of your life, and for that reason, needs to be taken seriously. But research has found that exercise can be an effective first line of defense against mild depression, equally as effective as some pharmaceuticals. For example, one study of 1,536 people found the odds of being depressed were three times lower among active people than among sedentary ones. Study after study shows that exercise reduces stress, decreases anxiety, improves self-esteem, and fights depression.

I recall a difficult time in my life when I was going through a divorce and feeling depressed. I just couldn't get myself out the door. My counselor recommended that I call my good friend Christee and tell her she needed to make me walk every day; she advised all her clients with depression to start walking. But I was a professional speaker on the subject! The thought that I needed a friend to force me to do something I get paid to talk about was a huge wakeup call for me. When you're down and

PENCIL TIME

Why Do You Want to Exercise?

In my WalkSport work, I often speak to large groups about physical fitness and the benefits of exercise. When I am done talking, I like to ask members of the audience why they exercise. I do this in part because I'm a curious person and interested in other people's lives. But I've also found that when we actually come out and state the reasons why we are exercising, we are actively converting *an* exercise program into *our* exercise program. When we start owning our program, we have an excellent chance of sticking with it.

So, find some paper and pick up a pencil—pencils have erasers that allow us the freedom to brainstorm, doodle, and eventually come up with exactly what we want. The rest, you erase. Plus, I figure that just about any idea looks good in a dazzling color of ink, but if it looks good in plain old graphite gray, you've got a good one.

Now, think about the real reasons why you want to exercise. Check off each statement that applies to you and add additional reasons in the space below.

__ I feel out of shape and want to become more fit.

__ I want to lose weight.

__ My doctor said I needed to start exercising.

__ I want to be more social and meet new friends.

even clinically depressed, it's so hard to motivate yourself or ask for support. Sometimes it's hard to see just how seriously down you are.

But then I resumed walking, and once I actually got up and moved again, my depression eased. Within just a few months of walking and more therapy, I felt back to my old self. Talking with my mall walking

---

___ I want more energy and to feel better in general.

___ I want to stop hurting.

___ I want to sleep better.

___ I want to improve my self-image.

___ I want to manage my stress better.

___ I want to look my best.

Additional reasons:

_____

_____

_____

_____

_____

Transfer your list of reasons onto a note card, written in ink (these are for real!). Carry the card with you at all times. Make copies and post them at places where you may need motivation: on your bedside table, the bathroom mirror, the refrigerator, your office desk, and your car's dashboard. Tap these cards for motivation at those times—and they will come—when you don't want to exercise. These reasons represent your highest aims—when you honor them, you honor yourself.

---

friends and observing thousands of mall walkers, I've discovered that my episode is all too common. Mall walking can do miracles for your mood.

Walking and Weight Loss

You know about the many *health* benefits of exercise, but what's the number one reason most of us start exercising to begin with? Say it with me: to lose weight.

We know that exercise is the key to losing weight, but just how does it work? Here's what mall walking does to help you whittle away your waist.

Burns calories. This number one benefit is a no-brainer. But beware! The principle of calories burned versus calories consumed becomes a very important issue if you "reward" yourself for the 300 calories you burned with a Coke and a bag of chips. That 10 minutes of snacking just wiped out your 30 minutes of walking.

One way to look at the calorie question is to use it as a balance for bad days, not a reward for good ones. I use mall walking to work off my "bad girl" days when I overeat. If I know I'm going to eat a lot at one meal, I make sure to schedule an extra long walk the next 2 days. That way, extra eating becomes a conscious decision to also spend more time making the rounds.

Builds muscle. Walking at a challenging pace, especially when you add in some strength training or the use of a PowerBelt, can help build muscle. Muscle cells are far more metabolically active than fat cells. Before you take even one step, each pound of muscle in your body burns 35 calories a day, versus a mere 2 calories for every pound of fat. Build more muscle, and you'll constantly be burning many more calories, even in your sleep!

Curbs your appetite. Don't forget what mom said—no walking with your mouth full. Typically, we don't tend to eat while we're exercising, and exercise seems to temporarily take the edge off hunger pangs. This appetite blunting can last for an hour or two after a workout. One of my first surprising discoveries about mall walking was that I ate less high-calorie foods, especially after I did challenging workouts. I *felt* healthier after a workout, so I wanted to *eat* healthier, too.

Adds pleasure, instead of subtracting it. With dieting alone, you are trying to lose weight by *eliminating* pleasures from your life. With exercise, in contrast, you are *gaining* an enjoyable activity.

Helps reduce stress. We know that exercise helps our bodies cope with stress, but many people turn to eating to handle stress. I know I'm guilty of that once in a while. (Okay, more than once in a while.) However, by exercising you can deal with the stress by *burning* rather than *adding* calories.

Increases confidence. You feel good during and after exercising because you are doing something positive for your life and your body. This feeling evolves into a belief that you *can* reach your weight loss goals, that it is entirely in your power. And once you have that power, there's no stopping you!

Eating Well to Maximize Weight Loss

As good as mall walking is for exercise, it's not the whole picture for weight loss. True, you'll come a long way by burning calories and building muscle, but you still have to pay attention to the principle of balancing the energy you take in with the energy you put out.

These two approaches—exercise and eating well—are like tag-team wrestlers. One of them is in the ring fighting fat, and then it tags the partner to finish the job. They work okay as individuals but are *great* as a team. I tried doing diets alone, and you know how that turned out. The only way I could lose weight and keep it off was by combining eating well with exercise.

This exercise-plus-eating-well approach is supported by decades of medical research. One compelling study found that 92 percent of people who were successful at maintaining their weight loss were getting regular physical activity. In the group that had gained back some or all of the weight they had lost, only 34 percent were still exercising. Not only is regaining weight a real downer, it can also be deadly. Past studies have shown that men and women who experienced a high degree of weight fluctuation were about twice as likely to die during the years following the study than those with stable weights.

The Seven Golden Rules of Eating for Weight Loss

Eating well for weight loss *doesn't* mean depriving yourself. We now know that the starvation mentality of years past is bad for you on every level: mentally, emotionally, and definitely physically. Today's smart mall walker is aware that knowledge is her ace in the hole. The more she knows about key nutritional principles, the better choices she can make, and the more weight she can lose—permanently.

I've absorbed mountains of books and articles on nutrition basics, and I've boiled it down to the guidelines that can help you get the healthiest, best results in the quickest amount of time. When you're done with this section, you'll know everything you need to know to manage your weight safely and effectively. We'll start with seven golden eating rules for mall walking weight loss.

1. Eat a variety of foods. For good health, you need more than 50 different nutrients classified into six groups: proteins, carbohydrates, fat, vitamins, minerals, and water. No one food can give you all groups, so it's not surprising that dietary variety is considered the single most important principle in nutrition. In terms of weight loss, eating a variety of foods allows you to get maximum nutrition from minimum calories. Research also shows that people who don't eat a variety of foods are at a higher risk of early death than those who eat from most or all of the groups.

In the 1950s, nutrition educators developed the Four Food Groups to encourage people to eat a variety of foods. Unfortunately, people considered each group as equal in importance and quantity (equal parts meat and potatoes, please!), so in 1992, the U.S. Departments of Agriculture and Health and Human Services introduced the Food Guide Pyramid as the new standard in nutrition education.

Like the Four Food Groups, the Food Guide Pyramid recommends variety, but it also offers specific recommendations for how much of each food group to eat each day. The pyramid divides foods into five main groups: grains group (bread, cereals, rice, and pasta), vegetable group, fruit group, milk group (milk, yogurt, and cheese), and meat and beans group (meat, poultry, fish, dry beans, eggs, and nuts). It gives specific recommendations of how much food to eat from each group a day. There is a sixth group—fats, oils, and sweets—at the top of the pyramid, but it's advised that you try to eat these foods sparingly. (For more on the Food Guide Pyramid, see page 45.)

2. Limit your total fat, saturated fat (the fat found in animal products), and cholesterol. While following this golden rule reduces your risk of heart attacks and certain types of cancer, it also automatically helps you maintain a healthy weight. Fat contains 9 calories per gram, more than twice the 4 calories per gram of carbohydrate and protein!

3. Eat plenty of vegetables and fruits. Plant foods provide essential vitamins, minerals, fiber, and complex carbohydrates without a lot of fat. These foods also have a lot of fiber to fill you up quickly—I know that when I eat my veggies and fruit, I have a lot less room for my cookies. The fiber in fruits and veggies also helps lower your risk of colon cancer and control your blood sugar levels.

4. Make whole grains a staple. Dishes made from grains, like wheat, rice and oats, provide essential vitamins, minerals, and carbohydrates, and they're generally low in fat. Whole grains like brown rice, oatmeal, and popcorn contain more fiber than the refined grains in white bread, pasta, and rice. These high-fiber foods also keep your belly full and your bowels moving along, so you won't feel bloated and uncomfortable when you walk.

5. Eat sugar in moderation. High-sugar diets are high in calories but low in nutrients. Nutritionists say that just by eliminating one can of soda from your diet each day, you could lose 15 pounds in a year. The average 12-ounce can contains 150 calories, but now it's more common to find 20-ounce bottles, which pack a whopping 250 calories each. Beware! As the container gets larger, so does the number of calories inside.

6. Limit your use of salt and sodium. A high–salt/sodium diet increases your risk of high blood pressure, counteracting the good work you're doing with mall walking. High salt intake also increases the amount of calcium your body loses through your urine, so eating less salt may decrease your risk of osteoporosis and bone fractures.

7. If you drink alcoholic beverages, do so in moderation. Alcohol packs a lot of calories with absolutely no nutritional upside. Plus, have you ever tried to turn down a plate of nachos or a pastry puff after a few glasses of wine? By dulling your resistance to temptation, alcohol can sabotage your best weight loss efforts.

These seven golden rules not only give you a great basis for weight loss, they also provide you with an overall understanding of good nutrition that can help keep you healthy and disease-free into your golden years.

Get All Your Nutritional Building Blocks

When I was dieting, I had weight management boiled down to this simple rule: Don't eat cookies. I don't know where I picked this up; maybe I had heard that sweets make you gain weight. Truth is, I really didn't know what I ate or, more accurately, what was in what I ate. I just ate it. Sara hungry, Sara eats. Perhaps you are the same way. To help you learn what's actually in the food you're putting into your mouth—so you can make the choice of whether it *should* be going into your mouth—let's cover the six building blocks of nutrition: proteins, carbohydrates, fat, vitamins, minerals, and water.

Let's say you go to the mall for a noontime walk. After your workout, your belly is empty and your head swims with visions of lunch. You head to the food court and decide that a sub from a sandwich shop would hit the spot.

Stop right there! All subs are not created equal. By learning a little bit about what nutrients your body will get *out of* your sandwich, you'll be better able to order the best things to go *into* your sandwich.

Say you request turkey, roast beef, cheese, lettuce, and tomato on a roll—a wonderful combination. Let's take a look at the building blocks that make up that sub and how you can make it even more nutritious and weight-loss savvy.

Protein. The turkey, roast beef, and cheese of the sub contain this important nutrient, found in every cell of your body. You can also get it in other meats, fish, dairy products, nuts, and legumes. Protein is essential because it allows the body to build and repair body tissues and, in a minor way, can be a source of energy. Protein is also used to make hemoglobin (part of red blood cells), antibodies (to fight off infections), and enzymes and hormones (which regulate body processes).

Best Weight Loss Bet: While roast beef may be tasty, you'd be better off doubling up on the turkey and limiting yourself to one slice of this red meat. Ounce for ounce, turkey has much less fat and fewer calories than beef, while still packing a powerful protein punch. Cheese doubles up as a source of protein and calcium, so by all means, include a slice or two, but stop there—it's also full of fat.

Carbohydrates. Your body will get the most energy from the sub's carbohydrates, which are found in the roll, the lettuce, and the tomato. Also found in other fruits, vegetables, grain products, and pastas, carbohydrates are the main source of energy for your central nervous system and red blood cells. Your body uses 20 to 25 percent more energy to metabolize carbohydrate than it does to metabolize fat, so higher-carbohydrate/lower-fat diets actually allow your body to burn extra calories during digestion.

Best Weight Loss Bet: The more complex the carbohydrates, the longer it will take for them to break down and the longer they will keep you feeling satisfied. Always ask if the sub shop offers whole wheat rolls and romaine lettuce—both will help you feel sated longer.

Fat. As I noted in the protein section, the cheese and roast beef are the primary sources of fat in your sandwich. But fat can also lurk in any toppings you put on the sandwich, like mayonnaise, dressing, or oil.

You hear a lot of bad things about fat, but it is an important nutrient. Fat supplies essential fatty acids, which are a crucial source of energy for muscles at rest and during light activity. Fatty acids also carry fat-soluble vitamins (A, D, E, and K) throughout the body, help prevent growth deficiencies, and build membranes in cell walls. Stored fat in the body protects vital organs, insulates against cold, and even acts as padding on your feet. And, as we know all too well, fat provides flavoring to many foods.

Fat's two types, saturated and unsaturated, are pretty easy to tell apart. Saturated fats are usually solid at room temperature and found in animal products, dairy products, and oils such as coconut and palm kernel. These known artery blockers have been linked to heart disease. No more than 10 percent of your total calories should be from saturated fats.

Unsaturated fats are usually liquid or soft at room temperature and are healthier than saturated fats. They are divided into monounsaturated (olive, peanut, and canola oils) and polyunsaturated (corn, safflower, soybean, and sunflower oils). Monounsaturated fats are considered the healthiest of the oils.

Best Weight Loss Bet: By far the best topping for your sub would be mustard—with no fat, mustard adds a piquant flavor for minimal calories. If you really need to have a little bit of fat, opt for an olive oil and vinegar dressing, emphasis on the vinegar—that way at least you'll get the healthy benefits of olive oil's monounsaturated fat. Whenever possible, avoid full-fat mayo. One tablespoon of mayonnaise, barely enough to cover the sub roll, tacks another 5 grams of fat onto your sandwich.

Vitamins. Vitamins are everywhere in your sub, and that's good because a variety of vitamins are vital. Vitamins help control the growth of all body tissues and are essential for the release of energy in the body. The sub's lettuce contains vitamin A, and the tomato has vitamins A and C. Thiamin is in the roll, and riboflavin and niacin are in the cheese, turkey, and roast beef.

Best Weight Loss Bet: Take full advantage of the sub shop's veggie tray: Ask for extra lettuce and tomato, and throw on some green peppers, onions, or even cucumbers for more vitamins C and A.

Here is a list of common vitamins and their functions.

- *Vitamin A* maintains eye and skin health and aids resistance to infection. Sources include carrots, sweet potatoes, margarine, and butter.

- *Vitamin B₁*, or thiamin, is needed so your digestive system, as well as your appetite, functions properly. It helps with functions of the nervous system, and aids in getting energy from carbohydrates. Some sources are grain products, meats, fruits, nuts, and vegetables.

- *Vitamin B$_2$*, or riboflavin, is used in energy metabolism, and it promotes good vision and healthy skin. You get this vitamin from milk products and meats.

- *Vitamin B$_3$*, or niacin, promotes healthy skin, helps your appetite, and aids in digestion and energy production from fats and carbohydrates. This vitamin is found in meat, fish, poultry, and grains.

- *Vitamin B$_6$* is used in protein and fatty acid metabolism, and it's needed for red blood cell formation. Meat, vegetables, and whole grains boast this important vitamin.

- *Vitamin B$_{12}$* is used in energy metabolism and the making of red blood cells and nucleic acids. Sources are meats, milk products, and eggs.

- *Vitamin C* strengthens body cells, promotes healing of wounds and bones, and increases resistance to infections. Get this vitamin from citrus fruits, green peppers, tomatoes, and other vegetables.

- *Vitamin D* aids in the absorption of calcium and therefore the growth and formation of bones and teeth. You can find this vitamin in eggs, tuna, and fortified milk.

- *Vitamin E* protects vitamins and essential fatty acids from destruction and therefore helps prevent cell membrane damage. This critical vitamin is found in vegetable oils, whole grain cereal and bread, and leafy green vegetables.

- *Folic acid* is used in making protein and nucleic acids. Sources include green vegetables, beans, and whole wheat products.

- *Vitamin K* is needed for blood clotting. You can get it from leafy green vegetables, peas, and potatoes.

Minerals. Minerals are important for body structure and play an important role in numerous key body functions. Your sub is no slacker here—the cheese offers calcium, and the roast beef and roll boast iron.

Best Weight Loss Bet: If you order a side of coleslaw, you'll instantly be boosting your calcium and phosphorus intake. Just make sure to steer clear of the fat-laden, mayo-based kinds—look for coleslaw prepared with vinaigrette instead.

Here are some key minerals and their functions.

- *Calcium* gives strength to your bones and teeth and helps your blood clot. It is also needed so that muscles, like your heart, contract and relax. About 99 percent of the calcium in the body is in the skeleton. Sources are milk, sardines, dark green vegetables, and nuts.

- *Iodine* aids thyroid hormone formation and therefore helps regulate the rate at which the body uses energy. Sources include iodized salt and seafood.

- *Iron* is an important part of hemoglobin, the part of the red blood cell that carries oxygen throughout the body. Iron is found in red meat, eggs, beans, leafy green vegetables, and shellfish.

- *Magnesium* helps regulate the use of carbohydrate and the production of energy within the cells. It also helps the nerves and muscles work. You can find this mineral in nuts, seafood, whole grains, and leafy green vegetables.

- *Phosphorus* combines with calcium to give bones and teeth strength and hardness. It is also involved in energy production. Sources include meat, poultry, seafood, eggs, milk, and beans.

- *Zinc* is a part of several enzymes that affect cell growth and repair. It is also part of insulin, which is essential for the use of glucose in the blood. Sources are meat, shellfish, yeast, and whole grains.

Water. Aside from scant traces in the veggies, the water content in your sub is negligible. That's certainly not the case in your body—about 60 percent of body weight is water. You may be able to survive a few weeks without food, but you'd only make it a few days without water. Water transports nutrients, gases, and waste products in the body and is important in heat regulation, yet most of us do not drink nearly enough. As a rule of thumb, drink about 4 cups of water for every 1,000 calories you eat. For most adults, that's about 8 to 10 cups (2½ quarts) of water each day.

Best Weight Loss Bet: Water is your best weight loss friend—it fills you up, prevents constipation and bloating, and keeps your digestive system running at maximum efficiency. Every time you come to the mall, bring a full liter bottle of water and stow it in a locker with your coat. If you drink to replenish the liquids you've lost during exercise, you may notice that you're not as ravenous and you can relax and savor your sub instead of wolfing it down!

Mall Walker's Map to the Food Pyramid

Okay, you have finished off your turkey and roast beef sub, and you have an idea of the nutrients you have eaten. Now I want to return to the Food Guide Pyramid, which I explained earlier, to see where your sub fits in.

As I said, the Food Guide Pyramid illustrates a nutritious diet and divides foods into five main groups. There is a sixth group—fats, oils, and sweets—at the top of the pyramid. Don't worry about eating your quota from this group because the recommendation is to eat these foods sparingly. Each group in the pyramid includes suggested daily servings that are listed. The food groups become a larger part of your diet as you move down the pyramid.

Many foods are a mixture from the five groups. That sub was made up of foods from four of the five main food groups: grain (roll), vegetable (lettuce, tomato), meat (turkey, roast beef), and milk (cheese). You must also include the fats and oils group because of the fat in the cheese and the meats as well as in the mayo or oil-and-vinegar topping that you added. (What, you thought condiments don't count?) The more you play around with this pyramid, the more second nature it will be to you. It won't take you long to start keeping track of what you eat and to break down combination foods into their components.

In the rest of this section, I'll explain each group in the Food Guide Pyramid. I want you to become familiar with which foods go where in the pyramid so you can use it as a tool to manage your weight.

THE MALL WALKER'S FOOD COURT PYRAMID

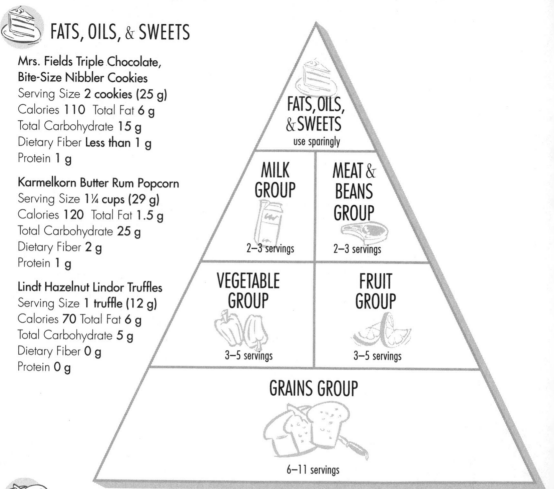

FATS, OILS, & SWEETS

Mrs. Fields Triple Chocolate, Bite-Size Nibbler Cookies
Serving Size **2 cookies (25 g)**
Calories **110** Total Fat **6 g**
Total Carbohydrate **15 g**
Dietary Fiber **Less than 1 g**
Protein **1 g**

Karmelkorn Butter Rum Popcorn
Serving Size **1¼ cups (29 g)**
Calories **120** Total Fat **1.5 g**
Total Carbohydrate **25 g**
Dietary Fiber **2 g**
Protein **1 g**

Lindt Hazelnut Lindor Truffles
Serving Size **1 truffle (12 g)**
Calories **70** Total Fat **6 g**
Total Carbohydrate **5 g**
Dietary Fiber **0 g**
Protein **0 g**

FATS, OILS, & SWEETS
use sparingly

MILK GROUP
2–3 servings

MEAT & BEANS GROUP
2–3 servings

VEGETABLE GROUP
3–5 servings

FRUIT GROUP
3–5 servings

GRAINS GROUP
6–11 servings

GRAINS GROUP

Auntie Anne's Whole Wheat Pretzel (without butter)
Serving Size **1 (this would count as 2 servings)** Calories **350** Total Fat **1.5 g**
Total Carbohydrate **72 g** Dietary Fiber **7 g** Protein **11 g**

Souper Salad Basil Pasta with Roasted Mushrooms
Serving Size **½ cup** Calories **112** Total Fat **4.4 g** Total Carbohydrate **15.6 g**
Dietary Fiber **Not available** Protein **Not available**

Manhattan Bagel Whole Wheat Bagel
Serving Size **1 bagel (4 ounces)** Calories **260** Total Fat **Less than 1 g**
Total Carbohydrate **52 g** Dietary Fiber **3 g** Protein **10 g**

MILK GROUP
(Milk, Yogurt, and Cheese)

Dairy Queen Fat-Free Frozen Vanilla Yogurt
Serving Size ½ cup (85 g)   Calories 100
Total Fat 0 g   Total Carbohydrate 21 g
Dietary Fiber 0 g   Protein 3 g

Starbucks Coffee Caffe Latte with Fat-Free Milk
Serving Size 16 ounces   Calories 160
Total Fat 1 g   Total Carbohydrate 21 g
Dietary Fiber 0 g   Protein Not available

TCBY Soft Serve Creamy Nonfat Frozen Yogurt
Serving Size ½ cup   Calories 110
Total Fat 0 g   Total Carbohydrate 23 g
Dietary Fiber 0 g   Protein 4 g
If served with 1 scoop fruit topping, add
10 additional calories and no fat;
this contributes to your servings of fruit.

VEGETABLE GROUP

Panda Express Mixed Vegetables
Serving Size 5 ounces   Calories 80
Total Fat 3 g   Total Carbohydrate 11 g
Dietary Fiber 2 g   Protein 1 g
Have **Panda Express Steamed Rice**
alongside (for a grain serving).
Serving Size 8 ounces   Calories 220
Total Fat 0 g   Total Carbohydrate 48 g
Dietary Fiber 1 g   Protein 5 g

Subway Veggie Delight Salad
Serving Size 1 salad (233 g)   Calories 50
Total Fat 1 g   Total Carbohydrate 9 g
Dietary Fiber 3 g   Protein 2 g

Schlotzsky's Tomato Florentine Soup
Serving Size 8 ounces   Calories 100
Total Fat 1 g   Total Carbohydrate 19 g
Dietary Fiber 1 g   Protein 14 g

MEAT & BEANS GROUP

Taco Bell Soft Beef Taco
Serving Size 3.5 ounces   Calories 210
Total Fat 10 g   Total Carbohydrate 20 g
Dietary Fiber 3 g   Protein 11 g

Chick-Fil-A Chargrilled Chicken Garden Salad
Serving Size 1 salad (9.8 ounces)
Calories 180   Total Fat 6 g
Total Carbohydrate 8 g   Dietary Fiber 3 g
Protein 23 g
Serve with 1 packet Light Italian Dressing,
which has 20 calories, 0.5 g fat, 3 g carbo-
hydrate, 0 g dietary fiber, 0 g protein in
1.25-ounce serving size.

Arby's Light Roast Turkey Deluxe (served on a multigrain bun)
Serving Size 7.2 ounces (1 sandwich)
Calories 260   Total Fat 5 g
Total Carbohydrate 33 g
Dietary Fiber 3 g   Protein 23 g

FRUIT GROUP

Au Bon Pain Freshly Squeezed Orange Juice
Serving Size 9 ounces   Calories 125
Total Fat Less than 1 g
Total Carbohydrate 27 g
Dietary Fiber 0.5 g   Protein 1 g

Mr. Bulky's Treats and Gifts Raisins
Serving Size 1.5 ounces   Calories 129
Total Fat Less than 0.2 g
Total Carbohydrate 34 g
Dietary Fiber 1.7 g   Protein 1.4 g

Orange Julius Bluberration Creation Drink
Serving Size 20 ounces   Calories 340
Total Fat 1 g   Total Carbohydrate 80 g
Dietary Fiber 5 g   Protein 2 g

Servings and Sizes

First, I want to explain two things about the pyramid: the range of servings that you see listed with each group, and what counts as a serving. In each range, the lower number of servings with each group supplies about 1,600 calories a day, while the higher number gives close to 2,800 calories a day. (Later in the book, on page 112, we will get into how many calories *your* body requires, but just remember that you can tailor this pyramid to your needs by changing the number of servings you eat.) Of course, these ranges assume you're sticking to the serving sizes, which can be kind of confusing. Take heart: Once you learn the system, it'll be the only one you need for lifelong eating.

The best way to learn the serving sizes for each food group is to take a few minutes to visualize them. For example, you may be overwhelmed by the thought of eating 6 to 11 servings in the bread group. But when you take a measuring cup and actually see what ½ cup of cooked rice or pasta looks like, it's not much, at least to me. The same is true with ½ cup of fruits or vegetables.

Here's an easy trick: To determine what an ounce of cereal looks like, take your 12-ounce box and pour the contents into 12 bowls, the same in each bowl. For cheese, cut an 8-ounce brick into eight equal pieces. Each one of them equals a serving. If you spend a few minutes now learning what the serving sizes look like, you'll be able to eyeball them forever.

Another way of remembering serving sizes is to associate them with familiar objects. Try making up your own associations. Here are a few to get you thinking.

- 3 ounces of meat, poultry, or fish = a deck of cards or cassette tape
- 1 ounce of hard cheese or 2 tablespoons of peanut butter = a ping pong ball
- 1 medium fruit or 1 cup of lettuce = a baseball

I know I'm a big visualization person. When I was first learning the pyramid, I found I was less willing to do the serving size thing when I had to futz around at every meal, measuring a serving of this or that. That's when I took 15 minutes to set up a full day's servings on my kitchen table. I laid out the foods I normally eat in each group and studied what counted as a serving. Right there in front of me, I laid out 6 to 11 servings from the bread group, 2 to 4 from the fruit, 3 to 5 from the vegetable, 2 to 3 from the meat, and 2 to 3 from the milk group. That's what I needed each day. I burned that image into my mind so that I had a visualization of my balanced, healthy diet. Since then, I've also found it very useful to carry a 3- by 5-inch "scorecard" so I can keep track of servings I eat from each food group throughout the day. Maybe you'll want to do something similar, either on an index card or in your day planner or journal.

A Stroll through the Food Groups

Let's start at the top of the pyramid and work our way down.

Fats, oils, and sweets. Nutrition experts say more than 40 percent of the calories in the average American's diet comes from fat. We eat so much fat because many prepared foods "hide" their fat, or we just love the taste of butter, cream, and oil—let's face it, fat adds flavor to food. I definitely watch what I eat, but my grease monsters, which bite me maybe three times a year, are onion blossoms and apple fritters. I love them. Pat Olson, R.D., a nutritionist in Burnsville, Minnesota, says that a certain high-fat Mexican burrito just buckles her knees with flavor. She says even the best of us indulge in fatty foods once in a while, but Pat is smart—she handles her slips by having no other fats for that day. Remember, total sacrifice is not the answer—occasional treats help you feel in control without feeling deprived.

Health groups like the American Heart Association recommend that no more than 30 percent of our calories come from fat, with saturated fat less than 10 percent of calories. Weight management experts often advise a further reduction to 20 percent for people trying to slim down.

So, how much fat should you consume each day? To find out, use your calculator to multiply 30 percent by your total number of calories for one day. (To find out how many calories you consume daily, see

"What Are You Eating?" on page 73.) Let's say you take in 2,000 calories each day. Multiply 2,000 by .30 and you come up with 600 calories as the upper limit for your daily fat consumption. How many grams of fat is that? To find out, divide 600 calories by 9 calories per gram of fat. This comes to 67 grams. For saturated fats, the process would be 2,000 calories multiplied by .10 equals 200 divided by 9 equals 22 grams. Check food labels to find out how many grams of fat and saturated fat are in each serving of the food you eat. Then add them up each day, and try to keep your total grams of fat below 67 grams and your saturated fat grams below 22.

Fats are found in every group on the Food Guide Pyramid. As you're learning about the pyramid, try to always check food labels to determine how much is fat. Pay more attention to the actual grams of fat than the package's claims, like "90 percent fat-free!" The percentage of calories from fat, what you calculated above, differs very much from these claims, which are based on weight. A hot dog, for example, may be listed as having 20 to 30 percent fat by weight because much of the hot dog's weight is from water, which has no calories. In reality, 70 to 80 percent of the calories of that hot dog are from fat!

I keep thinking of my friend Beth whom you heard about in chapter 1. You remember that she weighed 240 pounds when she started mall walking. Do you remember what dietary change she made to help her lose 100 pounds? She didn't go on a diet, she just cut out high-fat foods. Her experience confirms that cutting out high-fat foods is an excellent first step in maximizing your eating for weight loss.

There are oodles of ways to decrease the level of fat in your diet. For example, in the milk group you can use fat-free or low-fat milk (2 grams of fat) instead of whole milk (16 grams of fat). In the meat group, eat more fish, choose leaner cuts of meat, trim away visible fat and skin before cooking, broil or bake versus fry, and drastically reduce the number of processed meats you eat—they can be high in fat with extra additives and little nutritional value. Also, use nonstick pans and sprays for cooking. Fruits and vegetables are low in fat, unless you cover them in dressings, butter, or mayonnaise. Try substituting herbs, spices, or lemon juice, which could save you up to 9 grams of fat for each tablespoon of dressing. Similarly, there is little fat in the bread group. But hold the butter, which is 4 grams of fat per teaspoon. Many fresh breads taste good without the butter.

The other part of the tip of the pyramid is sweets. Sweets include sucrose (table sugar), brown sugar, raw sugar, glucose, dextrose, fructose, maltose, lactose (milk sugar), honey, syrup, corn sweetener, high-fructose corn syrup, molasses, and fruit juice concentrate. Chances are you will find one of these names on a food label, because sugars are everywhere.

Many nutritionists advise keeping processed sugar intake below 10 percent of your total daily caloric intake. So, if you eat 2,000 calories a day, this would come to 200 calories of sugar a day. Sugar, a carbohydrate, is 4 calories per gram, so that 200 calories is 50 grams of sugar (200 divided by 4). Food labels all tell how many grams of sugar one serving of the food contains, so it is easy to keep track of the number of grams of sugar you eat per day. Once you start paying attention to them, you'll see just how quickly they can add up!

Milk group (milk, yogurt, and cheese). These are good sources of protein, carbohydrate, and vitamins A, D, and calcium. But they are part of a package deal—and the other part is that some milk and cheese products contain large amounts of fat and cholesterol. Yogurt is another story. Fat-free or low-fat yogurt has good amounts of protein and carbohydrate, but they have far less fat than cheese and ice cream. Yogurt can be used as a substitute for sour cream and as an alternative in sauces and dressings. And, of course, haven't we all learned about the splendors of fat-free frozen yogurt?

Meat and legumes group (meat, poultry, fish, dry beans, eggs, and nuts). The foods in this group are excellent sources of protein, the B vitamins, iron, and zinc. Fish like salmon, herring, and mackerel are high in omega-3 fatty acids, which help fight against heart disease. Eskimos in Greenland have a diet high in fat and cholesterol and low in fruits, vegetables, and fiber. Nevertheless, they have a low incidence of heart disease because they eat a great deal of fish and therefore omega-3 fatty acids.

As with the milk and cheese group, some foods in the meat and legumes group can be high in fat, saturated fat, and cholesterol. Some of these foods include ham, ground beef, dark-meat chicken, and peanuts. Instead, look for poultry without skin, fish, and dry beans and peas—they are great sources of protein and other key nutrients, but they have less fat. Again, labels can help you navigate this maze. If meat, fish, or poultry is advertised as "lean," by law it must contain fewer than 10 grams of fat and fewer than 4 grams of saturated fat per 3-ounce serving. To be "extra lean," each serving must have fewer than 5 grams of total fat and fewer than 2 grams of saturated fat.

Vegetable group. Vegetables are low in fat and high in vitamins A and C as well as minerals such as iron. Packed with cancer-fighting antioxidants, vegetables can literally save your life. The more you eat vegetables, the less you eat fatty foods that can cause disease. Vegetables have gotten such a bad rap, starting from when we turned our noses up against them as kids. But the same kids who revolt against eating broccoli grow up to be parents who say to their kids: "You cannot leave the dinner table until you eat your vegetables." So out of rebellion, we never learn how to love these miracles of nature.

One of the biggest hurdles we have to get over is thinking that vegetables are boring. They're only bland if we allow them to be bland! Here are a few ways to make vegetables more appealing.

Try actually eating them. Many people have turned up their noses to vegetables based on one bad experience with a brussels sprout when they were seven. Try them again—this time with a sweet balsamic vinegar. Your taste buds have grown a lot more sophisticated than when you were a kid. Branch out and sample a variety, but always make room for the undeniable favorites. Fresh corn on the cob, anyone?

Grow your own. The process of planting, fertilizing, weeding, watering, and harvesting vegetables will make you appreciate the marvels of these nutritional powerhouses. I know I find that garden vegetables taste better. Home grown cherry tomatoes are like candy, and you have not tasted a real carrot until you taste one you've grown yourself.

Think presentation. Food that looks good can prepare our brains for thinking it tastes good. Use all the green, red, orange, and yellow vegetables—as well as their varied shapes—to present your dishes with dazzle.

Grill your veggies. Brush vegetables such as sliced zucchini and onions with a little olive oil, sprinkle on a few spices, and singe them on the grill. The smoky flavor adds a whole extra dimension to your vegetables.

Spice them up. Add herbs and other seasonings to steamed vegetables. A splash of lemon adds a little zing as well.

Try a blush of butter. Stir ½ teaspoon of butter through cooked vegetables. You get a great taste and hardly any fat.

Stir-fry. Throw just about any vegetables in a wok and, with the right sauce or seasonings, they will taste great. Besides, it is only fitting that after you walk, you wok!

Fruits group. Most people find it easier to eat fruits than vegetables, primarily because they're sweet. Fruits are low in sodium and fat and are a good source of fiber, but they also boast several minerals as well as lots of vitamins A and C.

Even with all these good things going for fruits, most Americans don't eat their 2 to 4 servings daily. Maybe they skip breakfast (a common characteristic among overweight people) and miss an opportunity to drink a glass of fruit juice or add fruit to their cereal instead of sugar. Maybe they tend to pass on fruits as snacks and pound down the pastries and chips instead. Maybe they find fruit not gooey or greasy—or sweet—enough for their tastes when they think about an appetizer or a dinnertime dessert.

To paraphrase John Lennon, all I am saying is give fruits a chance. They not only taste great and are good for you, but they help us lighten up, literally and figuratively. Often we take our meal planning too seriously, topping off a wonderful dinner with a weighty, disastrously rich dessert. Fruits are so tidy, shapely, self-contained, and full of light sweetness that they send people away from the table uplifted by the epicurean experience.

Grains group (breads, cereals, rice, and pasta). The old saying had the right idea: "Here is bread, which strengthens man's heart, and is therefore called the staff of life." The same can be said of cereals, rice, and pasta. It's no mistake that these foods, good sources of complex carbohydrates, low-fat energy, vitamins, minerals, and fiber, are the foundation of the pyramid.

The problem with foods in this group is that they can easily become "platform" foods—maybe you look at your slice of bread, bed of rice, or plate of pasta as a platform upon which you build a hut of high-fat toppings and spreads. As you eat your 6 to 11 servings from this group each day, beware of hidden fats as well as excess sugar and calories. They lurk in the spreads and toppings, but they can also be plentiful in bread, cookies, pastries, croissants, doughnuts, and cakes.

Since many of us cannot get excited about sitting down to a mound of plain rice or pasta, my advice is to serve toppings on the side so you can have a taste of them but not consume excess amounts. Also, use low-fat or low-calorie toppings, spreads, and sauces. With pasta stuffing and sauces that call for milk and cream, try using low-fat milk instead. If the pasta sauce or stuffing calls for meat, use lean meat with fat trimmed away. Drain all oil before throwing the meat in with the sauce.

Beyond Diet and Exercise: Other Factors in Weight Loss

The formula for weight loss is easy enough—burn more calories than you eat. The more calories you burn walking around the mall, and the fewer calories you take in at the food court, the more weight you will lose. But as any diet pro can tell you, sometimes it just isn't that simple in real life. When we take all the factors into account, some of the more hard to define complexities of weight loss arise. These factors include:

Metabolism. I am sure you have that one friend who can eat anything she wants and never gain an ounce, while you seem to pack on the pounds just *looking* at food. Scientists might say that you have a more efficient metabolism because a little bit of food goes a long way for you.

Because your metabolism doesn't burn calories as fast as your friend's, the excess turns to fat. However, you can console yourself with this: If a famine were to hit, your friend would be among the first to perish and you would be among the last. *Ha!* you think. *Lucky me.*

Genetics. If you are overweight, go through your family photo albums. Chances are many of your relatives are overweight as well. Sometimes, it's just all in the family. Research has found that if neither parent is overweight, their child has less than a 20 percent chance of being overweight. If one parent is overweight, the chances increase to 40 percent. If both parents are overweight, the percentage increases to 80 percent. Genes are a factor, so if everyone in your family is stocky, it's time to accept the fact that you may never be reed thin. On the other hand, don't throw in the towel on losing weight just because your family is overweight. Genetics is just one factor in weight loss.

Family and cultural influences. I have a Scandinavian friend whose family serves dinner and then "a little lunch" at about 9 P.M. The grandmother emerges from the pantry with a tray groaning with sandwiches and pastries—which had better be consumed lest Grandma's feelings be hurt. I'd wager it's more than a little tough to lose weight in that household. Family upbringing and cultural influences are powerful factors in weight loss because they are so deeply ingrained. When food has been the focus of family life, it can be very difficult to change those patterns when you're trying to shed pounds.

Psychological factors. I once knew a woman who, when times got tough, would drop everything at the door at home, rush to the refrigerator, pop the top on a tall container of cottage cheese, and dig in. It wasn't long before the container was empty. She said the cool, smooth treat calmed her down. (Luckily for her, it was low-fat cottage cheese and not high-fat ice cream!)

When stress, anger, loneliness, depression, anxiety, and other disturbing emotions rule the day, some people crave comfort foods, using them as a self-medication for their pain. Learning how to cope with the underlying problem, rather than reaching for food to stifle the emotion, is the first step in breaking your addiction to comfort foods.

These are some of the major factors in weight loss. Understanding

PENCIL ✏️ TIME

Why Do You Want to Lose Weight?

Meeting goals is always a matter of motivation. If you have strong reasons for losing weight, you are more likely to be successful. At any given time, about a quarter of men and almost half of women are trying to lose weight. Most cite health and appearance as the two greatest incentives. But what's in it for you? What are *your* reasons to lose weight?

Jot down seven reasons why you want to lose weight. They all don't have to be "should" reasons that meet universal approval, like for your health. It may be that you want to lose weight so your spouse will stop nagging you, or so you look good in a swimsuit. Often when you complete your list and analyze it, those "silly" reasons lead to insights into your real motivation for losing weight.

1. _____
2. _____
3. _____
4. _____
5. _____
6. _____
7. _____

You may have found it a breeze to fill out the first four or five reasons but were scratching your head with the last two or three. If you can't come up with seven, try this. Put a 10-pound weight or two 5-pound bags of sugar in a backpack. Now, wear the backpack wherever you go for a few hours. At first, the extra weight may seem like no problem. But in time it will slow you down, tire you out, and tick you off. In this frame of mind, it shouldn't be hard to remember how much easier life would be without carrying around those extra 10 pounds. I guarantee you will be able to find your seven reasons.

these factors will help you appreciate the full challenge of what you are up against in weight management and keep you from getting discouraged when you experience setbacks. No matter what your individual issues are, mall walking can help you achieve your weight loss goals.

Just 8 Pounds?

The WalkSport Fit Forever Program is a powerful combination of exercising and eating well that will help you lose 8 pounds in 8 weeks. "Big deal," you may say. "I've done crash dieting programs before that promise 8 pounds lost in 2 weeks—or less."

Yes, but this is not your standard yo-yo plan—you won't be losing this weight only to gain it back next month after getting back on solid foods. This weight will be gone for good, without starving yourself to keep it off.

What I aim to show you is that slow and steady progress toward a desired weight, at a rate of 1 to 2 pounds a week, is the safest, most permanent, and easiest way to maintain weight loss. You may even lose more with the WalkSport Fit Forever Program, but the important thing is getting acquainted with the taste of success with predictable, steady weight loss. You will gain confidence from finally understanding *exactly* what it takes to lose weight and continue to manage your weight long after my 8-week program ends.

In this chapter I have given you some of the basics of exercise and weight management. You will learn about other aspects as you read on, but I want to emphasize that you have a better chance of succeeding with weight management and gaining fitness when you have background information. When you know the basis for the program, the whole thing makes more sense and becomes easier to follow.

Now we'll move on to one of my favorite chapters, all about the most exciting part of the WalkSport program: motivation to change. I love seeing what happens to people when they make the commitment to better health through mall walking. Read on for quizzes that help you see how ready you are to begin, and then gather strength from the inspiring tips I've learned from my dearest mall walking friends.

3

The Motivated Mall Walker

"Revolutions are not made; they come. A revolution is as natural a growth as an oak." Wendell Phillips, an anti-slavery abolitionist, wrote this in the years leading up to the Civil War, but I believe it's still true today. Right now, a burgeoning revolution is growing inside you, the same kind of revolution Beth started to experience when one simple walk in the mall with friends led to a cascade of changes, including losing 100 pounds. But no one is going to force this personal revolution upon you. Encourage, yes. Motivate, yes. Force, no. The change will come from within you.

Change is not easy, and it's always easier if you *want* to change. You may have heard the saying, "When the student is ready, the teacher appears." After years of failing at diets and exercise programs, I was ready for a change to mall walking. The teacher who appeared for me was my son, when he asked me why I kept dieting even though it had never worked. Yes, learning to change what I ate and how I exercised was work. But I was ready for that challenge, because I recognized that I was tired of failure and pain. Knowing why I wanted to change made the work that much easier.

My hope is that this book has "appeared" in your life because you are ready for change. If that's the case, I'm excited to be a part of your switch to better health. This chapter will motivate you to get on the "change train" and keep on rolling.

If you're not ready, this chapter will help you realize that, too. I don't want to put you through 8 weeks of the WalkSport Fit Forever Program if you're not mentally ready for it yet. Going through the motions is a waste of your time and a setup for failure. But take heart—just reading this book is a sign that you're on the right path. At the very least, this chapter can help you discover *why* you are not ready and what it will take to make you ready.

Your state of readiness can shift, sometimes very quickly. Even if you are not ready now for my program, don't automatically think you must spend years wandering in the wilderness thinking big thoughts before you will finally be ready. No. Just one question from my son made me realize that now was the time for change. The same could happen to you—in a week or a month—and this program, and your mall, will be here when it does.

The Path of Change

Your change of lifestyle may be catalyzed by a combination of desire and timing, but once initiated, the process of your change will be very predictable. Change comes in stages—six of them to be exact. These stages, developed by James Prochaska, Ph.D., at the University of Rhode Island and Carlo DiClemente at the University of Houston, have been used successfully for years in helping people learn how to exercise, quit smoking, overcome eating disorders, and even kick alcoholism. Knowing and making good use of these stages of change can improve your chances of success with my WalkSport Fit Forever Program.

As you read through the following six stages, try to place yourself somewhere in this process. You may be closer to change than you think!

1. Precontemplation. At first glance, this hardly seems like a state of *change*. In this stage, you are probably thinking there is nothing you need to change—you don't need mall walking or to manage your weight at all—or you are still blaming someone or something else for your problems. You avoid talking about weight loss or exercise, and when you are forced to discuss these topics, you become defensive.

But change may be in the wings. You may notice that people express concern about your weight, for example. Your doctor may make a comment. You may have an accident or some sort of rude awakening regarding your health that gets you thinking. Some big event like a 40th birthday, 25th anniversary, or your retirement may give you pause and even frighten you. You may become more aware of yourself and your lack of exercise or your excess weight.

MALL WALKING MAVEN

Bob Transformed His Life

Bob's story is a classic case of transitioning from precontemplation to contemplation—and beyond. He was kind of hit-and-miss with his exercising (more on the miss side) until he faced a grim doctor who told him his blood pressure and cholesterol levels were too high. Changes would have to be made. Bob's doctor prescribed blood pressure medication and more exercise. So, he worked out at his worksite health center and walked his dog. It helped, but not enough to put a smile on his doctor's face.

So Bob started mall walking, and, after his retirement, walked 20 hours each week. "It's the people at the mall, mostly," says Bob when asked what motivates him to walk so much. "They are great. Now going to walk is automatic—like going to work, only more fun."

Two years of mall walking finally brought a smile to Bob's doctor's face. Bob's total cholesterol dropped 70 points, his blood pressure fell to 121/55 mm Hg, and he was completely free of blood pressure medication. He also lost 30 pounds.

2. Contemplation. In this stage, you start to ponder the possibility of a different way of being. You are open to the idea of mall walking and weight loss but not ready to plunge ahead. You seek new information, try to alter your understanding of the problems and how they affect your health, and ask for feedback from people you trust. You weigh the pros and cons of making a change, which can cause emotional responses that can sometimes be intense.

Contemplation may last for several months, as you reappraise your personal values, picture yourself with and without the change, anticipate the emotional experiences of the new you, and define your mall walking and weight management goals. At the end of contemplation, you feel ready to make a decision.

3. Preparation. Here, you make a conscious choice about change. You may decide you're still not quite ready to begin, but again, don't look at this as a failure. You're setting the stage for the time when you are ready to change. Take notes and use them when it feels right to move ahead.

On the other hand, you may make the commitment to change in this stage. After contemplating the situation, you believe you can do mall walking and weight management. So you map out a course of action, planning small, achievable steps with an understanding of the sacrifices you have to make. You define your goals even more precisely than you did in the contemplation stage. As you prepare, you let go of your past, imagine yourself being different in the future, feel willing to give time and energy to reach your goals, enlist the support of others, and set a start date.

4. Action. This is it, your new beginning! But this stage is much more than "just do it." You actually change the factors that have prevented you from mall walking or weight management in the past. You develop new behaviors, such as assertiveness, to help you hold firm in your resolve. You counter old, negative self-talk with new supportive affirmations (see "Use Affirmations to Stay on Track" on page 66 for more on affirmations). You begin to learn how to avoid places, situations, and people that have caused you to overeat or be a couch potato, and you restructure your environment to avoid high-risk (or high-temptation!) situations. Finally, you reward yourself for each achievement along the way and continue to ask others for support and encouragement.

5. Maintenance. This stage is critical to your success—it's the one in which you escape the "take-a breather-after-a-major-achievement" trap. How many of us have lost weight only to have it come back on when we're "done" with our diet? Maintenance is the important step that will help you keep focused and not have a relapse.

In this stage, you continue your action plan, including giving yourself rewards. You've learned how to watch out for social pressures, internal "just this once" temptations, stress, and problematic situations. You continue to build on your success of the action stage by adding to your support system, reinforcing the positive lifestyle that goes with your new self-image, and even helping someone else start a weight loss and mall walking program. If you slip, you understand that slips happen. You remember the improvements you have made and keep going with your new life, all the while being patient with yourself.

6. Recycling and termination. Recycling is an ongoing stage of maintenance that includes the normal lapses and conscious recommitments to change. Recycling can actually be a lifelong stage of tweaking this and that aspect of your program. You may ask yourself questions like:

- Was this lapse a one-time thing or the result of an ongoing problem?
- Is it time for me to devote more time and money, maybe buy a light cookbook or a mall walking gadget?
- Am I really up-to-date on new information that can help me?
- Would a conference or a getaway reinvigorate me?
- What would happen if I started over from the beginning and went through the stages of change again, with beginner's eyes?

It's important to see recycling not as just the same old same old or, worse, as a failure. Each time you recycle, you develop a new degree of mastery. Take me for example: Even though I've been walking for many years, I recently realized I haven't been pushing my speed much. That realization made me see that I may have lost some ground in my fitness level. Does this mean I've failed? No way. I've come a long way, baby, and I just need to change my workouts a little by increasing my speed. I'm not starting over, just becoming a wiser mall walker.

Termination is the point at which your change is second nature. You feel no temptation to go back to your high-fat diet or to stop mall walking. You have a solid sense of your power and your change to a healthier lifestyle.

The Importance of Optimism

As you encounter each stage of change, you'll start to understand the importance of attitude. Making the changes necessary to follow a mall walking and weight management program can be difficult at times, but a can-do approach always makes the challenge easier.

When I think optimism I think of Suzanne. Before she became a mall walker, Suzanne took a fitness walking class. She was so excited about

PENCIL TIME

Replacing Negative Thoughts

Write down your two most common pessimistic thoughts about exercise.

_____

_____

Now write down optimistic thoughts to replace those pessimistic thoughts.

_____

_____

walking that she decided to forgo riding the bus to and from work each day. She walked instead, even though the winter months in Minnesota can be brutal. As the winter wore on, Suzanne says she was shocked to discover that "the fat was just melting away." She lost 15 pounds and was overjoyed. She was so up and energized by her walks that even her coworkers noticed. Suzanne was amazed at how the change in her walking had affected her attitude about work and life.

What I like about Suzanne is that she stayed on the left side of "but." We all make statements like, "I want to lose weight, but. . ." Or, "Gee, I'd like to do mall walking, but. . . ." Too often, we give more weight to what comes after the "but" than the more positive statement that comes before it. The "but" acts as an excuse that overrides the desire, the "I want to" part of the statement.

Suzanne and other can-doers focus on the left side of "but." She had plenty of excuses for not walking, including freezing weather and time pressures to get to work. However, she, like other optimists, doesn't waste a lot of energy on rationalizations but instead puts her energy into finding ways to get it done. She believes that negative emotions tend to narrow thinking, whereas positive emotions broaden the range of possibilities that help to build strength, resilience, and confidence.

One year, I made a New Year's resolution to walk every day, no matter what. I was doing fine until I was scheduled to have a surgical procedure. I thought, "Oh, great! Now how am I going to get in my walk and stick to my resolution?" I whined a bit until I decided to change my attitude. I put my energy into finding a way to fit walking in however I could. The surgery was a same-day procedure, so I decided to walk very early before I left for the surgery center. The solution, at least for that day, was simple once I became more optimistic.

Developing a sense of optimism *always* helps you with weight management and exercise, and a growing body of research is showing how it can help you live longer, too. Between 1962 and 1965, the Mayo Clinic asked 839 people to answer psychological questions that defined their outlook on life. When studied later, a retrospective look revealed that the most pessimistic among them tended to die earlier than the most optimistic, regardless of age or sex. In fact, every 10-point increase in the pessimism scale that researchers developed resulted in a 19 percent increase in premature death.

The study was yet another layer in the groundswell of support for the theory that optimism leads to increased health and longevity, as well as success at work, school, sports, and other goals. And when I look around the mall walking community, I see that I am surrounded by optimists. But don't just take my word for it—go to a mall and observe mall walkers. Talk to them. Walk with them awhile. Chances are you'll quickly detect their upbeat nature. Does mall walking make them optimists, or are optimists drawn to mall walking? I don't think anyone knows, but that's one chicken-and-egg argument that's pointless to debate. The upshot is, optimism and mall walking go hand-in-hand, no matter what starts first.

I firmly believe that any one of us can develop thinking habits that lead to—and preserve—a sense of optimism. Whether we work on this while walking in the mall, or making our way through the rest of our day, the choice is ours. Here are ten ways to bring more optimism into your life.

1. **Focus on solutions,** not on problems.

2. **Focus on what you *do* want,** not on what you *don't* want. Rather than telling yourself "I don't want to be fat" say instead "I want to be fit."

3. **Avoid "emotional vacuum cleaners,"** people who suck good feelings right out of you by saying things like, "You want to lose how much? Ha! Fat chance!" Be ruthless—just weed these people out of your life.

4. **Keep a straight posture.** Good posture not only helps create the physical presence of an optimist, but it will help you become a more efficient, stronger walker. More about that later.

5. **Vent.** When things look bleak, allow yourself 5 minutes to verbalize your negative thoughts, perhaps to a friend. Get it out of your system, but keep the venting to a predetermined length of time. Don't drone on and on.

6. **Reframe.** Choose to look at even the most mundane events in a favorable light. Instead of looking at going to the mall for a walk as one more to-do to cross off your list, think of it as an opportunity to clear your head so you can return to the office fresh.

7. **Applaud when you do something well.** Put your hands together, and give it up for YOU! Conversely, when something unfortunate happens, don't dwell on it.

8. **Schedule fun.** Plan positive events well in advance. Anticipating them—a walk and lunch with a friend, for example—brightens your mood and your sense of optimism.

9. **Keep a gratitude journal,** writing entries of things you are grateful for every day. An attitude of gratitude helps you see how much you have and gives you evidence that the future is probably going to be more of the same.

10. **Act as if.** Imagine you have lost those 20 pounds and are mall walking daily. Seeing yourself as successful, especially when things are tough, will help bolster your confidence in your abilities, and your optimism. Albert Camus once wrote: "In the depths of winter, I finally learned that within me there lay an invincible summer." Do everything you can to support your own invincible summer within.

Use Affirmations to Stay on Track

According to the Tao de Ching, the words you use to express your inner thoughts are the seeds of your future experiences. This image makes perfect sense to me, so I try to express myself with "seeds" that will grow into life-affirming thoughts and attitudes. Affirmations are simple statements made up of positive words that can be powerful tools for change.

Sadly, we often sabotage our dreams—sometimes unconsciously—with a constant barrage of negative self-talk. We make sarcastic comments to ourselves ("Nice move, loser!") that we would never say to someone else. Or we torpedo our goals before we even begin, tripping ourselves up with "Brother, this will never work!" comments. Affirmations cut through that negativity, help us see that positive events are possible, encourage us to become our own best supporters, and remind us we have a right to our dreams. As you go through the changes that accompany the WalkSport Fit Forever Program, affirmations can help ease your transition from one stage to the next—I urge you to use them as often as possible.

At first, you may pooh-pooh affirmations. Wrapped up in the tangle of complex problems, you may find yourself dismissing these seemingly simple statements with backtalk like, "Who do you think you're kidding?" As unnatural as they may feel, stay with them. Affirmations are not self-deception, but self-direction. You will find that you'll begin to like the way they make you feel. These simple, strong, positive cheers are portable and easy to use, and best yet, they reflect a dream that already is coming true. If optimism ensures success, and the heart of optimism is believing in yourself, affirmations can be your keys to that success.

In the space on page 68, jot down five affirmations to launch your mall walking and weight management program. Memorize and repeat them many times throughout your day. Here are some suggestions on how to create affirmations.

Use the present tense. Affirmations are much more powerful when they are spoken as if they are happening now, as in "I can do this," or "I have the resolve to reach my goals." They are even more effective if you visualize what the affirmation is stating as you recite it.

Be positive. Throwing a big old NOT in a statement à la "I will not overeat today" does little to inspire you and may even awaken the rebel within. Instead, quiet the rebel with calm positives like "I will eat lightly today."

Make it short. Brevity means you will actually use the affirmation. You will have a harder time remembering one that is overgrown with verbiage.

Be rhythmic. People like cadence and rhyme, so use them to help make an attractive affirmation. "Positive thinking will stop me from sinking."

YOUR AFFIRMATIONS:

_____

_____

_____

_____

_____

Where Do You Stand Now?

Poised on the edge of success, you've arrived at an exciting point in the book. The following tests assess how ready you are to do my WalkSport Fit Forever Program. Many people freeze up when they see the word "test," but not to worry—you can't fail here. These test results will not be published in the newspaper, with MY SCORES printed in boldface type. These tests are merely tools to help determine where you are in terms of diet and fitness. It's hard to figure out where you're going if you don't know where you are. So take these tests, and if you are overcome by one of those old college final-exam freak-outs, slap it down with a few of your new affirmations. Record your scores in a diary or journal, so you can track your progress. (For more information on using diaries, see chapter 4.)

The first tests help you discover if you are overweight. You may have a pretty good idea already, but take these tests to be sure. According to the National Heart, Lung, and Blood Institute (NHLBI) guidelines, assessment of overweight involves three key measures.

Body mass index (BMI). This measure is a simple ratio of your weight relative to your height. The BMI replaced the old height/weight guidelines because it is more accurate for most adults regardless of age, frame, or muscle mass. (However, it may not be very accurate for athletes who may have more extreme muscle mass, or pregnant or nursing mothers, whose bodies are supporting two beings. Also, the safe BMI range for those who may be frail may not be accurately reflected in this chart.)

To find your BMI, you'll need a calculator, pencil, and paper. First, divide your weight (in pounds) by the square of your height (in inches). Multiply that figure by 704.5 to arrive at your BMI.

For example: Say you are 5 feet 9 inches (69 inches) and weigh 140 pounds. To estimate your BMI, first you must find 69 squared. Do this by multiplying 69 by 69, which equals 4,761. Next, divide your weight, 140, by 4,761 and you get 0.0294. Multiply 0.0294 by 704.5, and your BMI equals 20.71.

$$[\text{Your Weight} \underline{\qquad} \div (\text{Your Height})^2] \times 704.5 = \underline{\qquad} (\text{Your BMI})$$

Take this score and locate it within one of the ranges below.

BMI SCORING

Underweight	Below 18.5
Normal	18.5 to 24.9
Overweight	25 to 29.9
Obese	Above 30

Waist circumference. This test is an easy one—simply place a tape measure snugly around your waist and see where the end touches. Very important: As tempting as it may be, do not hold your breath, or "suck it in." To make sure you're getting an accurate reading, once you have a measurement, take a full breath and allow the tape to expand to accommodate your breathing.

This measurement is a good indicator of your abdominal fat, which is a predictor of your risk for developing risk factors for heart disease and other diseases.

Check the table below to find out where you stand in terms of your waist circumference.

WAIST CIRCUMFERENCE SCORING

Risk	Men	Women
Low risk	Waist circumference under 40 inches	Waist circumference under 35 inches
Increased risk	Waist circumference over 40 inches	Waist circumference over 35 inches

Risk factors for diseases and conditions associated with obesity. This chart puts your BMI together with your waist circumference to give you a better idea about the degree of your risk for developing obesity-associated diseases or conditions.

RISK OF TYPE 2 DIABETES, HIGH BLOOD PRESSURE, AND CARDIOVASCULAR DISEASE

	BMI	Obesity Class	Men <40-inch waist	Men >40-inch waist	Women <35-inch waist	Women >35-inch waist
Underweight	<18.5					
Normal	18.5–24.9					
Overweight	25–29.9		Increased		High	
Obese	30–34.9	I		High		Very high
Obese	35–39.9	II		Very high		Very high
Extremely Obese	40+	III		Extremely high		Extremely high

In addition to the BMI and waist circumference, additional risk factors for developing disease are often related to, if not directly attributable to, being overweight. These include:

- High blood pressure
- High LDL cholesterol
- Low HDL cholesterol
- High tryglycerides
- High blood sugar
- Family history of premature heart disease
- Physical inactivity
- Cigarette smoking

For people who are considered obese (BMI greater than or equal to 30) or those who are overweight (BMI of 25 to 29.9) and have two or more risk factors, the NHLBI recommends losing weight as soon as possible. People who are overweight, do not have a high waist measurement, and have fewer than two risk factors may not need to lose weight, but instead focus their efforts on weight management and preventing any further weight gain. Talk with your doctor to see if you are at an increased risk and if you should lose weight. Your doctor will evaluate your BMI, waist measurement, and others risk factors for heart disease.

As indicated in the list above, people who are overweight or obese have a greater chance of developing high blood pressure, high blood cholesterol or other lipid disorders, type 2 diabetes, heart disease, stroke, and certain cancers. Even a weight loss as small as 10 percent of your current weight will help to lower your risk of developing these diseases. Following the WalkSport Fit Forever Plan is designed to safely help you shed at least 10 percent of your body weight at a rate that will help you keep it off for life.

(Note: If these tests indicate that you are underweight, please talk to your doctor as well to get a clean bill of health before beginning the WalkSport plan.)

Are You Ready to Get Started?

After taking the above tests to see if you are overweight, you may finally feel ready to lose weight. But are you *really* ready? The following tests will help you make sure.

Nutritionists Pat Olson, R.D., and Kay Guidarelli, R.D., created this readiness test especially for the WalkSport Fit Forever Program. Pat is a nutritionist and a certified diabetes educator at Quello Clinic in Burnsville, Minnesota, and Kay is a consultant and dietitian in Minneapolis, Minnesota. These 15 simple-but-probing statements give you feedback about your readiness. The test is intended for people who have their physician's approval to do a weight management program. It is not intended for people with eating disorders such as anorexia nervosa and bulimia.

The WalkSport Weight Management Readiness Test

For each statement answer:

Strongly agree = 1

Somewhat agree = 2

Neutral = 3

Somewhat disagree = 4

Strongly disagree = 5

The number you've assigned to each response is the point or points you will receive for that response. When you are finished with the test, add up your points and use the scale below to determine whether you are ready for weight management.

_____ This is a lifelong change, not a temporary diet.

_____ My weight loss process will be slow and more permanent, not fast and temporary.

_____ I believe exercise should be a part of a weight management program.

_____ I am motivated to make mall walking a high priority and fit it into my daily schedule.

_____ I have, or am willing to obtain, the resources I need, such as shoes and transportation, to do mall walking.

_____ In order to begin mall walking, I am willing to search for a mall that is right for me.

_____ I am doing this not just to lose weight but also because I want stress relief, social time, enjoyment of exercise, time for myself, and/or better health in general.

_____ I am willing to make changes in my diet and lifestyle to support my mall walking program.

_____ I am ready to lose weight, to "see" myself carrying fewer pounds.

_____ I have clear weight management and mall walking goals and take full responsibility for reaching those goals.

_____ I believe that reading food labels is important in weight management.

_____ I am willing to look at potential emotional factors involved in my eating behavior and to address these factors.

_____ I am ready to eat three moderate meals a day and reduce my intake of fatty foods.

_____ I would have no problems doing a mall walking workout three times this week.

_____ I understand that a mall walking and weight management program alone cannot change me; it is up to me to do that, and only I can benefit from the changes.

TOTAL SCORE: _____

If you scored:

15–30: You are ready.

31–45: You are close to being ready, but you still have reservations.

46–60: You are not ready. Go back to your 3, 2, and 1 responses, and build on these strengths.

61–75: You are not ready. Go back to the Pencil Time exercises you did in chapter 2 on why you want to exercise and manage your weight. Pay attention to your responses on this test— they'll tell you what you need to do to become ready for this program.

What Are You Eating?

In chapter 2, you learned that good nutrition is essential to managing your weight. Take this Rate-Your-Diet Test to evaluate your nutrition. The test was developed by the Center for Science in the Public Interest in Washington, D.C.

The questions below will help you focus on the important factors of your diet. The (+) or (-) numbers under each set of answers instantly pat you on the back for good habits or alert you to problems you may not even realize you have. This test doesn't attempt to cover everything in your diet. The test focuses on fat, saturated fat, cholesterol, sodium, sugar, fiber, and vitamins A and C, without drilling down to precise measurements of how much of these nutrients you eat. What the test does is give you a rough sketch of your current eating habits and indications of what you can do to improve them.

Rate-Your-Diet Test

Take out a sheet of paper and write down the numbers 1 through 39. For each question of the test, each answer corresponds to a number that shows a plus or minus sign in front of it. You can either circle the number in the book or write the number down on your sheet of paper. That number is your score for each question.

For each question, circle the number or numbers that apply to you, averaging two or more scores if necessary. Here's how to average: In question 19, for example, if your sandwich eating is equally divided among tuna salad (-2), roast beef (+1), and turkey breast (+3) on a typical day, add the three scores (which gives you +2) and then divide by 3 (the number of responses you gave). That gives you a score of +⅔ for the question. If averaging gives you a fraction, round it to the nearest whole number. So, round up +⅔ to +1.

Pay close attention to serving sizes, which we give when needed. For example, a serving of vegetables is ½ cup. If you usually eat 1 cup of vegetables at a time, count it as two servings.

When you're done, add up all your (+) scores and your (-) scores. Subtract your (-) scores from your (+) scores. When you have your grand total, check it against the key at the end. Your rating will help you evaluate the quality of your overall diet, on a scale from "Co-o-ol" to "Oops!"

After 8 weeks on the Walksport Fit Forever Program, take the test again and compare your scores to see the progress you've made.

THE TEST

Fruits, vegetables, grains, and beans

1. How many servings of fruit or 100 percent fruit juice do you eat per day? (Omit fruit snacks like Fruit Roll-Ups and fruit-on-the-bottom yogurt. One serving = one piece or ½ cup fruit or 6 ounces fruit juice.)

   a. 0 = –3

   b. less than 1 = –2

   c. 1 = 0

   d. 2 = +1

   e. 3 = +2

   f. 4 or more = +3

2. How many servings of nonfried vegetables do you eat per day? (One serving = ½ cup. Include potatoes.)

   a. 0 = –3

   b. less than 1 = –2

   c. 1 = 0

   d. 2 = +1

   e. 3 = +2

   f. 4 or more = +3

3. How many servings of vitamin-rich vegetables do you eat per week? (One serving = ½ cup. Count broccoli, Brussels sprouts, carrots, collards, kale, red pepper, spinach, sweet potatoes, or winter squash *only*.)

   a. 0 = –3

   b. 1 to 3 = +1

   c. 4 to 6 = +2

   d. 7 or more = +3

4. How many servings of leafy green vegetables do you eat per week? (One serving = ½ cup cooked or 1 cup raw. Count collards, kale, mustard greens, romaine lettuce, spinach, or Swiss chard *only*.)

   a. 0 = –3

   b. less than 1 = –2

   c. 1 to 2 = +1

   d. 3 to 4 = +2

   e. 5 or more = +3

5. How many times per week does your lunch or dinner contain grains, vegetables, or beans, but little or no meat, poultry, fish, eggs, or cheese?

   a. 0 = –1

   b. 1 to 2 = +1

   c. 3 to 4 = +2

   d. 5 or more = +3

6. How many times per week do you eat beans, split peas, or lentils? (Omit green beans.)

a. 0 = –3   d. 2 = +1
b. less than 1 = –1   e. 3 = +2
c. 1 = 0   f. 4 or more = +3

7. How many servings of grains do you eat per day? (One serving = 1 slice of bread, 1 ounce crackers, 1 large pancake, 1 cup pasta or cold cereal, or ½ cup granola, cooked cereal, rice, or bulgur. Omit heavily sweetened cold cereals.)

a. 0 = –3   d. 5 to 7 = +2
b. 1 to 2 = 0   e. 8 or more = +3
c. 3 to 4 = +1

8. What type of bread, rolls, etc., do you eat?

a. 100 percent whole wheat as the only flour = +3
b. whole wheat flour as the first or second flour = +2
c. rye, pumpernickel, or oatmeal = +1
d. white, French, or Italian = 0

9. What kind of breakfast cereal do you eat?

a. whole grain (like oatmeal or Wheaties) = +3
b. low-fiber (like Cream of Wheat or Corn Flakes) = 0
c. sugary low-fiber (like Frosted Flakes) or low-fat granola = –1
d. regular granola = –2

Meat, poultry, and seafood

10. How many times per week do you eat high-fat red meats (hamburgers, pork chops, ribs, hot dogs, pot roast, sausage, bologna, steaks other than round steak, etc.)?

a. 0 = +3   d. 2 = –2
b. less than 1 = +2   e. 3 = –3
c. 1 = –1   f. 4 or more = –4

11. How many times per week do you eat lean red meats (hot dogs or luncheon meats with no more than 2 grams of fat per serving, round steak, or pork tenderloin)?

a. 0 = +3

b. less than 1 = +1

c. 1 = 0

d. 2 to 3 = –1

e. 4 to 5 = –2

f. 6 or more = –3

12. After cooking, how large is the serving of red meat you eat?

a. 6 ounces or more = –3

b. 4 to 5 ounces = –2

c. 3 ounces or less = 0

d. don't eat red meat = +3

13. If you eat red meat, do you trim the visible fat when you cook or eat it?

a. yes = +1

b. no = –3

14. What kind of ground meat or poultry do you eat?

a. regular ground beef = –4

b. ground beef that's 11 to 25 percent fat = –3

c. ground chicken or 10 percent fat ground beef = –2

d. ground turkey = –1

e. ground turkey breast = +3

f. don't eat ground meat or poultry = +3

15. What chicken parts do you eat?

a. breast = +3

b. drumstick = +1

c. thigh = –1

d. wing = –2

e. don't eat poultry = +3

16. If you eat poultry, do you remove the skin before eating?

a. yes = +2

b. no = –3

17. If you eat seafood, how many times per week?

a. less than 1 = 0

b. 1 = +1

c. 2 = +2

d. 3 or more = +3

Mixed foods

18. What is your most typical breakfast? (Subtract an extra 3 points if you also eat sausage.)

     a. biscuit sandwich or croissant sandwich = –4

     b. croissant, Danish, or doughnut = –3

     c. eggs = –3

     d. pancakes, French toast, or waffles = –1

     e. cereal, toast, or bagel (no cream cheese) = +3

     f. low-fat yogurt or low-fat cottage cheese = +3

     g. don't eat breakfast = 0

19. What sandwich fillings do you eat?

     a. regular luncheon meat, cheese, or egg salad = –3

     b. tuna or chicken salad or ham = –2

     c. peanut butter = 0

     d. roast beef = +1

     e. low-fat luncheon meat = +1

     f. tuna or chicken salad made with fat-free mayo = +3

     g. turkey breast or hummus = +3

20. What do you order on your pizza?

     a. no cheese with at least one vegetable topping = +3

     b. cheese with at least one vegetable topping = –1

     c. cheese = –2

     d. cheese with one meat topping = –3

     e. don't eat pizza = +3

21. What do you put on your pasta? (Add 1 point if you also add sautéed vegetables.)

     a. tomato sauce or red clam sauce = +3

     b. meat sauce or meat balls = –1

     c. pesto or another oily sauce = –3

     d. Alfredo or another creamy sauce = –4

22. How many times per week do you eat deep-fried foods (fish, chicken, french fries, potato chips, etc.)?

a. 0 = +3

b. 1 = 0

c. 2 = –1

d. 3 = –2

e. 4 or more = –3

23. At the salad bar, what do you choose?

a. lemon, vinegar, or no dressing = +3

b. fat-free dressing = +2

c. low- or reduced-calorie dressing = +1

d. oil and vinegar = –1

e. regular dressing = –2

f. cole slaw, pasta salad, or potato salad = –2

g. cheese or eggs = –3

24. How many times per week do you eat canned or dried soups or frozen dinners? (Omit lower-sodium, low-fat ones.)

a. 0 = +3

b. 1 = 0

c. 2 = –1

d. 3 to 4 = –2

e. 5 or more = –3

25. How many servings of low-fat calcium-rich foods do you eat per day? (One serving = ⅔ cup low-fat or fat-free milk or yogurt, 1 ounce low-fat cheese, 1½ ounces sardines, 3½ ounces canned salmon with bones, 1 ounce tofu made with calcium sulfate, 1 cup collards or kale, or 200 milligrams of a calcium supplement.)

a. 0 = +3

b. less than 1 = –1

c. 1 = +1

d. 2 = +2

e. 3 or more = +3

26. How many times per week do you eat cheese? (Include pizza, cheeseburgers, lasagna, tacos or nachos with cheese, etc. Omit foods made with low-fat cheese.)

a. 0 = +3

b. 1 = +1

c. 2 = –1

d. 3 = –2

e. 4 or more = –3

27. How many egg yolks do you eat per week? (Add one yoke for every slice of quiche you eat.)

    a. 0 = +3   d. 3 = −1

    b. 1 = +1   e. 4 = −2

    c. 2 = 0   f. 5 or more = −3

Fats and oils

28. What do you put on your bread, toast, bagel, or English muffin?

    a. stick butter or cream cheese = −4

    b. stick margarine or whipped butter = −3

    c. regular tub margarine = −2

    d. light tub margarine or whipped light butter = −1

    e. jam, fat-free margarine, or fat-free cream cheese = 0

    f. nothing = +3

29. What do your spread on your sandwiches?

    a. mayonnaise = −2

    b. light mayonnaise = −1

    c. ketchup, mustard, or fat-free mayonnaise = +1

    d. nothing = +2

30. With what do you make tuna salad, pasta salad, chicken salad, etc.?

    a. mayonnaise = −2

    b. light mayonnaise = −1

    c. fat-free mayonnaise = 0

    d. low-fat yogurt = +2

31. What do you use to sauté vegetables or other foods? (Vegetable oil includes safflower, corn, sunflower, and soybean.)

    a. butter or lard = −3

    b. margarine = −2

    c. vegetable oil or light margarine = −1

    d. olive or canola oil = +1

    e. broth = +2

    f. cooking spray = +3

Beverages

32. What do you drink on a typical day?

> a. water or club soda = +3
> b. caffeine-free coffee or tea = 0
> c. diet soda = –1
> d. coffee or tea (up to 4 a day) = –1
> e. regular soda (up to 2 a day) = –2
> f. regular soda (3 or more a day) = –3
> g. coffee or tea (5 or more a day) = –3

33. What kind of "fruit" beverage do you drink?

> a. orange, grapefruit, prune, or pineapple juice = +3
> b. apple, grape, or pear juice = +1
> c. cranberry juice blend or cocktail = 0
> d. fruit "drink," "ade," or "punch" = –3

34. What kind of milk do you drink?

> a. whole = –3   c. 1% low-fat = +2
> b. 2% fat = –1   d. fat-free = +3

Desserts and snacks

35. What do you eat as a snack?

> a. fruits or vegetables = +3   d. cookies or fried chips = –2
> b. low-fat yogurt = +2   e. nuts or granola bar = –2
> c. low-fat crackers = +1   f. candy bar or pastry = –3

36. Which of the following "salty" snacks do you eat?

> a. potato chips, corn chips, or popcorn = –3
> b. tortilla chips = –2
> c. salted pretzels or light microwave popcorn = –1
> d. unsalted pretzels = +2
> e. baked tortilla or potato chips or homemade air-popped popcorn = +3
> f. don't eat salty snacks = +3

37. What kind of cookies do you eat?

    a. fat-free cookies = +2

    b. graham crackers or reduced-fat cookies = +1

    c. oatmeal cookies = –1

    d. sandwich cookies (like Oreos) = –2

    e. chocolate-coated, chocolate chip, or peanut butter = –3

    f. don't eat cookies = +3

38. What kind of cake or pastry do you eat?

    a. cheesecake = –4

    b. pie or doughnuts = –3

    c. cake with frosting = –2

    d. cake without frosting = –1

    e. muffins = 0

    f. angel food, fat-free, or fat-free pastry = +1

    g. don't eat cakes or pastries = +3

39. What kind of frozen dessert do you eat? (Subtract 1 point for each of the following toppings: hot fudge, nuts, or chocolate candy bars or pieces.)

    a. gourmet ice cream = –4

    b. regular ice cream = –3

    c. frozen yogurt or light ice cream = –1

    d. sorbet, sherbet, or ices = –1

    e. fat-free frozen yogurt or fat-free ice cream = +1

    f. don't eat frozen desserts = +3

Scoring your diet

Add up your scores for all questions to determine your Grand Total. If your score is:

0 or below then	OOPS!	Your diet needs to improve ASAP
1 to 29	HMMM.	Don't be discouraged; start incorporating changes slowly
30 to 59	YESSS!	Congratulations, you're well on your way.
60 or above	CO-O-OL	No room for improvement—you're eating a great diet!

Are You Ready for Exercise?

Becoming more active is very safe for most people. However, some people should check with their doctor before they start becoming much more physically active.

If you plan to become much more physically active than you are now, answer the questions below. If you are between the ages of 15 and 69, the Physical Activity Readiness Questionnaire (PAR-Q) will tell you if you should check with your doctor before you start. If you are over 69 years of age and you are not used to being active, check with your doctor.

Common sense is your best guide when you answer these questions. Please read the questions carefully, and answer each one honestly, selecting YES or NO.

YES NO   1. Has your doctor ever said that you have a heart condition and that you should only do physical activity recommended by a doctor?

YES NO   2. Do you feel pain in your chest when you do physical activity?

YES NO   3. In the past month, have you had chest pain when you were not doing physical activity?

YES NO   4. Do you lose your balance because of dizziness or do you ever lose consciousness?

YES NO   5. Do you have a bone or joint problem that could be made worse by a change in your physical activity?

YES NO   6. Is your doctor currently prescribing drugs (for example, water pills) for your blood pressure or a heart condition?

YES NO   7. Do you know of any other reason why you should not do physical activity?

If you answered YES to one or more PAR-Q questions, talk with your doctor by phone or in person *before* you start becoming much more physically active or *before* you have a fitness appraisal. Tell your doctor that you took the PAR-Q and point out which questions you answered YES.

- You may be able to do any activity you want—as long as you start slowly and build up gradually. Or, you may need to restrict your activities to those which are safe for you. Talk with your doctor about the kinds of activities you wish to participate in and follow his or her advice.

- Find out which community programs are safe and helpful for you.

If you answered NO honestly to *all* questions, you can be reasonably sure that you can:

- Start becoming much more physically active—begin slowly and build up gradually. This is the safest and easiest way to go.

- Take part in a fitness appraisal—this is an excellent way to determine your basic fitness so that you can plan the best way for you to live actively.

In some cases it's best to delay becoming much more active.

- If you are not feeling well because of a temporary illness such as a cold or a fever, wait until you feel better.

- If you are or may be pregnant, talk to your doctor before you start becoming more active.

Please note: If your health changes so that you then answer YES to any of the above questions, tell your fitness or health professional. Ask whether you should change your physical activity plan.

Informed use of the PAR-Q: The Canadian Society for Exercise Physiology, Health Canada, and their agents assume no liability for persons who undertake physical activity, and if in doubt after completing this questionnaire, consult your doctor prior to physical activity.

Assessing Your Fitness

To reap the maximum health benefits from exercise, you need to make strides on several fitness frontiers. Fitness has four components.

- *Cardiorespiratory fitness* is the heart's ability to pump blood and deliver oxygen throughout your body.
- *Muscular fitness* is the strength and endurance of your muscles.
- *Flexibility* refers to your ability to move your joints freely and without pain through a wide range of motion.
- *Body composition* is the concern for the portion of your body weight made up of fat.

I must tattle on many of my mall walking friends. They think they're fit because they walk and therefore cover the cardiorespiratory fitness component. Nope. The four components are like streams that feed the river of health. Without flexibility, for example, movement can be limiting, painful, and even disabling. Exercise without regard for body fat can lead to joint problems, obesity, and heart disease. I am happy to say that the WalkSport Fit Forever Program includes all four components of fitness.

In most fitness books, we would probably take the time now to determine your fitness level for each component. But I am not going to put you through all of these tests, and I will tell you why.

I have no problems with certain fitness tests. For example, the BMI and waist circumference tests you took were a relatively painless way to give you a look at your body composition. Similarly, the flexibility test (see "How Flexible Are You?" on page 87) is not time consuming and is easy to perform. Results from these tests will help motivate you as you make progress through the program. As I suggested before, keep a record of your results in a journal or calendar, then retake these tests after you finish the WalkSport Fit Forever Program—and perhaps every 2 months after that—and compare the results. Nothing builds confidence and a feeling of success more than proof of results!

What I *do* have problems with is self-testing for cardiorespiratory and muscular fitness. I'm not sure it's worth the risk. Let me tell you a quick story of why I prefer that you *not* take this test without proper medical supervision.

The cardiorespiratory test has been used extensively to determine cardiorespiratory fitness levels among walkers. This test is to be administered on a track or a measured mile. Test takers are told to warm up, stretch, and then line up at the starting point. Then they're instructed to start a stopwatch and begin walking. After 1 mile, they stop, check their watch, and record the time to the nearest minute, and then immediately take their pulses. Finally, test takers plot their results on fitness charts for men and women at various ages to compare individual results against national averages.

Test takers usually figure out that to do well (and who doesn't want to do well on any test?), they have to go as fast as they can for 1 mile without stopping to rest. These tests can easily turn into all-out efforts, which concerns me for any exercisers, especially beginners. My terrifying experience with this test was a great lesson in human nature.

During a presentation for a chiropractic clinic, I gave the cardiorespiratory test to a group of walkers. I remember telling people to listen to their bodies and not to "overdo it." At the end of the test, I assisted those walkers who had difficulty feeling their pulse. I was alarmed to find that a few of these people had seriously high pulses.

One of these walkers started to feel pain in his arm and asked for assistance from a chiropractor, who was nearby. With urging, the walker reluctantly agreed to go to the hospital. As it turned out, he was in the throes of a heart attack.

When I visited him later, he assured me that the incident was not my fault. He said he always overdid things, and that during the test he went flat out as fast as he could. He graciously reminded me of my warning at the beginning of the test not to overdo it.

His response gave me some relief, but then and there I decided to stop administering this test. I wasn't going to take that chance again. So instead of doing the cardiorespiratory and muscular fitness tests on your own, I recommend that you do them as part of your medical checkup.

How Flexible Are You?

Exercising and gaining strength both involve a lot of muscle contractions. These repeated contractions can shorten muscles over time, making them bulkier (which some people like) and tighter. But tight, knotty muscles are not pliable and adaptable. By being inflexible, these tight muscles can deprive the body of optimum health by inhibiting joint movement, causing misalignments in the body, decreasing body efficiency, and increasing the risk of injury.

My yoga friends explain it to me this way: A muscle action can be compared to a sponge. When you squeeze a sponge, it's like contracting a muscle. For the sponge to most effectively absorb fluids again, it must be fully released and become pliable. Our muscles are the same—in order for the contracted muscle to effectively contract again and again, as it does in movement of any sort, then it must be able to fully release and become pliable.

For most people, being flexible is the forgotten part of being fit. I don't want you to forget flexibility, especially as you age. When you are flexible, you move more easily and freely, you are less tense and subject to injury, you have an improved awareness of your body, and you just plain feel better. To begin, take the flexibility test below, and then keep taking it as you go through the WalkSport Fit Forever Program. You may be stiff at the start, so don't push yourself to overstretch. Just go slow, breathe normally, and be gentle with stretching—in no time, you'll become more limber.

The Modified Sit-and-Reach Test

To start this test, get a yardstick and a roll of adhesive tape. Place the yardstick on the floor with the zero mark closest to you. Tape the yardstick to the floor at the 15-inch mark, with the tape perpendicular to the yardstick.

Before doing the test, you'll want to warm your muscles up a little bit. Begin by walking slowly and then gradually increase your pace until you feel warm or begin to perspire. Then do a few easy stretches to loosen up your body. These include: a seated toe touch; a triceps stretch (gently pull one elbow and then the other above your head); a shoulder stretch (gently pull one elbow and then the other across your chest); upper body twists; a calf and hamstring stretch (while sitting on floor with knees bent, pull gently on your toes). (See the photos starting on page 120 for more stretches and explicit instructions.)

Now you are ready to do the modified sit-and-reach test. You may want to ask a friend to help you keep your legs straight during the test, but your friend cannot assist in or interfere with your movement.

Sit on the floor with the yardstick between your legs, your feet 10 to 12 inches apart, and your heels even with the tape at the 15-inch mark.

Place one hand over the other so the tips of your middle fingers are on top of one another.

Slowly stretch forward without bouncing or jerking. Slide your fingertips along the yardstick as far as you can reach. Go to the point where you feel mild tension, then relax and hold the stretch. Don't overstretch. Note where your fingertips touch the yardstick. (See photo, opposite page.)

Do the test three times. Record your best score to the nearest inch in your journal.

As I have said before, I am not all that enthusiastic about comparing your score to the national standards. If you'd like, you can stop right here and just repeat the tests later, noting your improvement. But if you'd like to see where you stand in comparison with others your age, use the table below.

MODIFIED SIT-AND-REACH SCORING

Men

Score at Age	20–29	30–39	40–49	50–59	60+
High	19 and over	18 and over	17 and over	16 and over	15 and over
Average	13–18	12–17	11–16	10–15	9–14
Below average	10–12	9–11	8–10	7–9	6–8
Low	9 or less	8 or less	7 or less	6 or less	5 or less

Score at Age	20–29	30–39	40–49	50–59	60+
Women					
High	22 and over	21 and over	20 and over	19 and over	18 and over
Average	16–21	15–20	14–19	13–18	12–17
Below average	13–15	12–14	11–13	10–12	9–11
Low	12 or less	11 or less	10 or less	9 or less	8 or less

Source: American College of Sports Medicine

"Yeah, I Can Do This!"

Congratulations! You've worked through three chapters and you're perched on the edge of beginning your WalkSport Fit Forever Program. Before you turn the page and launch into Week 1, take a moment to read this inspiring list of ideas. Some may make you laugh, some may seem downright silly, but some will definitely motivate you to lace up your shoes, head for the mall, and say, "Yeah, I can do this!"

Visualize the New You. One way to get started with weight loss, fitness, or at any project is to visualize the end result and mentally experience the benefits up front. Imagine a "mirror of tomorrow," and picture yourself having benefited from months of mall walking and weight management. See your proud posture and firmer, leaner body that looks good in both street clothes and swimming suits.

Dress the part. Put your mall walking clothes on in the morning when you rise, and don't take them off until you've had your mall walking workout.

Make a date. Plan dinner for two and a movie at the mall—but give yourself time to take a good walk first.

Use the phone. Ask a friend or family member to call and remind you to head out to the mall for a workout.

And baby makes two! Take your infant or toddler for a stroll around the mall. (More about this in part III.)

Get out of the office. For lunch, eat at your favorite spot in the food court—but only after your mall walking workout.

Watch 10 percent less television. When you watch less TV, you're automatically being more active. Now, use that "found" time to go mall walking.

Listen while you walk. Okay, I'll admit it, cutting down on TV can be tough. Why not try a small handheld television or an AM/FM headset that picks up TV audio? The soaps never sounded so dramatic.

Stay in touch at the mall. You know that list of friends and family members you want to spend more time with? Once or twice a week, pick one person off that list and meet at the mall for a walk and talk.

Make *other* health goals. Make a commitment to yourself that your mall walking and weight management will also lower your blood pressure, cholesterol, or resting heart rate. Research shows it's possible.

Read on the "run." Have the best classics, like Tolstoy, Eliot, and Austen, read to you while mall walking with books on tape.

Tempt yourself with java. Promise yourself the best cup of coffee the mall has to offer—but only after you've had your mall walking workout.

Get your motor running. Or order a large cup of coffee and drink it all while reading the paper, then just try to sit still! You'll be careening around the mall with energy to spare.

Play "60 Minutes." Drive to the mall, do some shopping plus a 30-minute workout, and drive back to work—all in 1 hour exactly.

Bet a dollar. Place $1 in the foliage of an out-of-the-way potted plant. Then do a quick lap around the mall before someone finds the dollar. If you really want to up your speed, drop a $5 or $10 bill.

Become a dictator. Write a novel, article, or report while mall walking by dictating your thoughts into a micro-cassette recorder.

Save on your energy bill. On really cold days, turn down your house's thermostat and plan for a day at the mall. Do breakfast, read the paper or a book, finish a work project, do a mall walking workout, and then have a lunch date. Follow that up with a matinee movie or even a double feature, another stroll, and then dinner. (Also works on hot days of summer—save on air conditioning!)

Book it. Schedule your mall walking time in your planning book just as you do other important appointments. Don't let yourself down—be punctual and set start and finish times.

Accept accolades. If you are overweight and embarrassed to go mall walking, try imagining that everyone whom you think stares at you is really applauding with his or her eyes. Guess what? Most of them *do* give heavy people a great deal of credit for making an effort.

Buy a buddy brunch. Find a mall walking buddy and buy his or her brunch after your walk. Next time your buddy buys. Schedule buddy walk-and-brunch dates a month in advance, alternating who buys.

Embrace solitude. Any activity, like mall walking, that doesn't take concentration and isn't overly stimulating could be just what you need in order to relax, daydream, and unwind. I once met a woman who walked the skyways in downtown St. Paul on her lunch break. She adamantly re fused to let friends join her, calling her walks "my time." She lost 66 pounds!

Don't act your age. Take a kid with you on your mall walks, and do everything he or she does while you walk. Let him pull you around, peek in the fountains, make faces at the puppies in the pet shop window. Kids know how to burn a lot of energy while they have their fun!

Try transition times. Sometimes, Monday mornings before work or evenings after a busy day can be a real drag. Start off, or end, your hectic day with a quick walk at the mall—it's relaxing, invigorating, and helpful in transitioning your head to and from work. Do the same before and after vacations.

PENCIL ✏️ TIME

What Motivates You?

List five incentives to motivate you to go to the mall for your walking workouts.

1. _____
2. _____
3. _____
4. _____
5. _____

Walk in a smoke-free zone. If you smoke, think about the times of day that you always light up. Create a positive habit in place of the negative by substituting mall walking for smoking in those times (most malls are nonsmoking areas).

Play "I spy." Make up mall walking games. For example, walk as long as it takes to spot three pink sweaters in the window displays.

Delegate, then walk. Many of us suffer from the "I have to do it all myself" syndrome, either at home or at work. Delegate three things off your list, and use that time for mall walking.

Be a do-gooder. Walk at the mall until you can do three small acts of kindness for others. It could be something like picking up a dropped glove or helping someone find a store. The people you help will feel better, and so will you.

Walk until you laugh five times. People do funny things, and this will help you look for ways to lighten up.

Pretend today's walk is your last walk—ever. By living truly in the moment, you'll gain a sense of real appreciation for your walk, your mall, and your life!

Part II

The WalkSport Fit
Forever Program

Week 1: Setting Goals

Welcome to the WalkSport Fit Forever Program. What an exciting time! The pretests and explanations are over, and the moment of truth has come—it's time to lace up your shoes and hit the mall.

Your goals for this week are easy. I don't want you to lose a pound (nor gain any, either), I'd like you to start a food diary (but don't change the way you eat, yet!) and I want you to walk three times at the mall. That's it. Choose when you'd like to go, and walk at whatever pace you want for as far as you want. My main aim for these critical first steps is to strip away any potential barriers that you may have to starting a mall walking program. I want your first week to be a slam dunk.

Each week, we'll dig deeper into some of the concepts I introduced in part I, to help you see how you can custom-tailor the Fit Forever Program to *your* life and *your* goals. And speaking of goals, because setting concrete, specific goals is the key to achieving your dreams, we'll begin right there.

GOALS FOR WEEK 1:

• Mall walk three times, any length

• Lose 0 pounds

Set Your Sights on Success

In a convenient, easy-to-spot bubble at the beginning of each week of the WalkSport Fit Forever Program, you'll find your mall walking and weight management goals for that week. Having them stated so explicitly may be different for many of you—most people begin exercise programs with hazy goals like "I want to get in shape," or even with no goals at all. Very often, these are the same people who give up when they see no evidence of progress. That's the beauty of concrete and specific goals: You can gauge your progress and celebrate gains in health, no matter how small.

A goal is an image of something you desire, but it's also a fixed point that feels good to work toward. Dreams live in your mind and heart—and they will stay there forever unless you translate them into goals. As author Leo B. Helzel said, "A goal is a dream with a deadline."

Meeting goals helps you be who you want to be, boosts your self-confidence and self-reliance, encourages you to trust your decisions, and generally gives you tremendous satisfaction. Try the following suggestions on setting and reaching goals from Bev Bachel, author of *What Do You Really Want? How to Set a Goal and Go for It!*

Set an achievable goal. Dream big, but make your goal something possible to realize. "I want to wear a size 6" might not be realistic for you, but "I want to walk 6 days a week, eat according to the Food Pyramid, and lose 25 pounds" might be. Always try to make your goals measurable, as in "I want to tighten my belt one notch tighter" or "I want to lower my cholesterol 10 points."

Set intermediate goals. Smaller, interim goals are stepping-stones to your big goal. If your big goal seems dauntingly large, first break it up into two, then four, then six goals, again and again until each intermediate step seems possible. Try to break it down to its smallest essence, even if that means daily goals—in fact, daily goals are usually the most achievable of all.

One easy way to track your intermediate goals in relation to your big goal is to create a goal ladder in your journal. At the top of the ladder write your ultimate goal with the date you wish to accomplish it. Write an intermediate goal in each rung of the ladder along with dates you want to accomplish them. Once you have created your goal ladder, sign your name, sealing this deal with yourself. Then start to climb that ladder!

Record your goals. Setting goals can be easy—but forgetting them can be even easier. Write your goals down and review them daily, weekly, or monthly, or as often as needed to keep them fresh in your mind.

Date your goals. Pegging your goals to specific dates will give you reference points that will help you keep track of your progress. Looking back on the dates, you'll be amazed at how much you have accomplished.

Create a vision. Make a collage of what you are striving for, so you can think in pictures instead of words. Collect photos of yourself, cut-out magazine pictures, and other objects (like old dress labels or driver's licenses) that reflect a thinner or healthier you, and glue them to a piece of posterboard. Place it where you can see it every day—visualizing your success helps you believe that you can reach your goal. If you *believe* you can do it, you *will* do it.

Go public. Spread the word about your goals to family and friends. They can help you stay on track and encourage you along the way. Making your plans public pulls the goal out of your head and into reality. When I told my son Peter that I would never go on a diet again, the resolution took on more meaning and made me more committed.

Put procrastination in the past. Setting goals usually brings about a bit of procrastination. It's natural for our fear of change to get in the way temporarily. Break through procrastination by taking 10 minutes right now to work on your goal. Don't wait until you have a huge block of time to get started. You can get a lot done in 10 minutes—and then you probably won't want to quit. In mental preparation for your mall walk, take a walk around the block, block out your three mall sessions in your calendar, or even just lay out the clothes you'll wear walking tomorrow—every small step is a signal to yourself that you're making progress.

Put perfectionism in the past. When we set out to make goals, many of us decide we're going to go all-out and not let ourselves slide this time. While this drive is admirable, it's also paralyzing. Rather than trying to be perfect, strive to get a "C+" in goals. You don't need an "A+"— you just need to get going.

Concentrate on effort, not outcomes. As you go along, you may become discouraged, thinking things aren't happening as quickly as you'd like. Take comfort—every day, you are getting healthier and closer to your goals. Instead of getting down on yourself, focus on what is in your control, and just keep up the good effort.

Try to remember this story about a student who worked with a master potter: One day, the student picked up one of the master's pots to admire it. He fumbled and dropped it, and it broke into pieces. The master smiled and said, "Don't worry. The pot is still there." The teacher was saying that the physical pot had been merely the goal that had enabled him to experience the delightful process of creating it. The pot was still "there," because the experience was still with him.

Sometimes we can become too attached to our goals, which creates tension and makes it difficult to get into the process. When we're distanced from the process, we enjoy it less. Whatever your mall walking and weight management goals are, they will come and go. The *process* of changing your lifestyle to one that is healthier is what will endure.

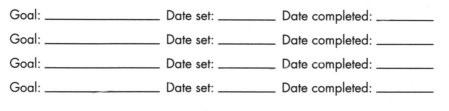

PENCIL TIME

What Are Your Goals?

Make a list of your mall walking and weight loss goals. After each goal, record today's date and the date you want to accomplish your goal. Create goal ladders for listing the intermediate goals pertaining to each goal you write here.

Goal: _____ Date set: _____ Date completed: _____

Goal: _____ Date set: _____ Date completed: _____

Goal: _____ Date set: _____ Date completed: _____

Goal: _____ Date set: _____ Date completed: _____

Get a goal buddy. Having a goal buddy can be the best thing you can do in reaching goals. Meet with a friend regularly to discuss goals. She can hold you accountable and encourage you, and you can return the favor. Moving toward goals can be frustrating, and you may be sorely tempted to ditch all the determination you had coming into the process. A good goal buddy will be there to lift your chin and help you recommit to your goal.

Reward yourself along the way. Celebrate not only your successes but also your efforts. Be creative and try to tailor your rewards to things that you know will make you truly happy. Nonfood rewards are especially satisfying and important when you are trying to manage your weight. Reflect on why you are rewarding yourself, and then let it soak in. Think about what Walt Disney said: "It's kind of fun to do the impossible."

How Hard, How Long, How Often

This week your mall walking goal is to walk three times at the mall at whatever pace you want and for however long you want. In coming weeks, you will gradually increase the frequency, duration, and intensity of your mall walks, and so I want to explain these terms and why they are important factors in exercise.

Frequency

Frequency is a measure of how *often* you mall walk. Many beginners tend to focus on two other factors, intensity and duration, thinking they have to go hard and long to get a training effect. That couldn't be further from the truth. Frequency is just as, or maybe more, important as intensity and duration. I would rather see someone mall walking almost every day at a lesser pace, versus going full bore for a long time just a few days a week. Your risk of injury is lower, and you enjoy it more. Plus, the more frequently you exercise, the quicker it will become a habit. You should not approach mall walking, or any form of exercise, as if you were trying to smash your way through an enormous wall. Instead, think of exercise as a pleasant way to coax a continual flow of positive feelings from your body.

Duration

Many mall walkers who have been at it awhile find this factor to be almost a nonfactor. They don't even think about how long they are going to walk; they just go to the mall and do their normal 30 to 45 minutes, which is long enough for a good workout.

This amount of time is also long enough to get into a nice rhythm. In the first 10 minutes or so of my mall walks, I shed the hassles and tensions of my day like a snake does his worn-out skin and get into a pleasant zone of reflection. Reflection enables me to take time out and check in with myself, without the continual distractions of the day. How is my body doing? My mind? My soul? Reflection takes time and practice, and the more you do it the more you will like both it and mall walking. If you walk on your own willingly, appreciating the time alone with your thoughts, you'll come to enjoy your inner journeys and be grateful that mall walking is an activity that allows for reflection.

That said, many beginners might walk for shorter durations and wonder if they are getting any health benefits. Studies show that they are, especially if they have been sedentary. Recent research shows that three 10-minute walks are just about equivalent to one 30-minute walk in terms of health benefits. So, if you cannot carve out a half hour for walking, take short walking breaks and get about the same effect.

Intensity

When reading about the recommended intensity of exercise, many mall walkers find words like "briskly" or "vigorously" a bit vague. They wonder, *Just how fast do I have to walk to get benefits?* They want a tool that can help them define intensity more precisely.

I was startled to read a survey of 7,500 adults in Michigan that showed only 25 percent of them walked fast enough to be in the "brisk walking" category. I'll bet the people not in the "brisk walking" category were also startled and vowed to pay more attention to their intensity. But it's equally likely that you're walking briskly enough, and you just don't know it.

I'll never forget one couple that I met when I was a presenter at a mall health fair. I was one of eight health specialists giving health tips, positioned at different booths throughout the mall. Attendees to the fair made loops around the mall, walking "briskly." When they passed certain checkpoints, an official punched a card, which was then used in a drawing.

Everyone was getting into the act and having fun, and many people stopped at my booth for information on mall walking, but I kept noticing one couple that consistently passed me. When I beckoned them over, they said, "No, we're not walking fast enough to be part of the health fair." I asked permission to take their pulses and told them that, indeed, their pace was strong enough to give them fat-burning, heart-strengthening benefits from their walk. Their faces lit up.

I know it can be very satisfying to learn that you're mall walking at an intensity that makes for a good workout. Here are three ways to measure your workout intensity.

Target heart rate (THR). This is actually a range of heart rates within which you should aim for an effective aerobic workout for your age. THR is based on your maximum heart rate, which you calculate by subtracting your age from 220. Why 220? At age 20, your average maximum heart rate is 220 beats per minute. As you age, your maximum heart rate gradually drops. Scientists have found this to be the *average* maximum, so yours (when you were 20) may have been slightly more or less. Basically, the maximum heart rate is a good ballpark estimate.

For healthy people, their THR is 60 to 80 percent of maximum heart rate. So, if you are 30, your max is 190 $(220 - 30)$ and your THR is between 114 $(.60 \times 190)$ and 152 $(.80 \times 190)$. Using the same calculations, you can figure your THR according to your age. Or, instead of doing the math, just check out this chart.

TARGET TRAINING ZONES

AGE	ZONE
20	120–160
25	117–156
30	114–152
35	111–148
40	108–144
45	105–140
50	102–136
55	99–132
60	96–128
65	93–124
70	90–120
75+	87–116

The easiest, cheapest way to measure your heart rate is by taking your pulse. Count your heartbeats at your wrist or neck for 10 seconds, and then multiply that by 6.

Or, you can measure your heart rate with a heart rate monitor. These gadgets, which can cost $80 and up, provide instant, constant feedback on your intensity, and you don't have to stop to take your pulse. You can set most heart rate monitors to beep at the heart rate that corresponds to the high and low end of your THR.

Once you have determined your THR, check from time to time during your mall walks to see if you are working out in that range. If your heart rate is below, pick up your pace. If it's above, slow down or risk injury or tiring too quickly. Gradually increase your heart rate within your range as you become more comfortable with mall walking.

Rate of perceived exertion (RPE). The key word is "perceived." You rate how hard you are working by using your own perception of how fast your heart is beating, how much you are sweating, how hard you are breathing, and how fatigued you feel.

Developed in the 1970s, RPEs have been shown by scientists to be rather accurate evaluations of how hard your body actually is working. That is, if the mall walking feels too difficult or too easy, it probably is— and is not a very satisfying workout to you.

With RPE, you simply take an inventory of your body—your legs, lungs, heart, arms, sweat—as you are mall walking. Then look at the chart below and assign a number to how you feel.

RATE OF PERCEIVED EXERTION

RPE	How It Feels
6–8	Very, very light exertion
9–10	Very light
11–12	Moderate
13–14	Somewhat hard
15–16	Hard
17–18	Very hard
19–20	Very, very hard

Determining RPE requires practice because you are setting the standards of "moderate" or "somewhat hard," which are subjective and vary from day to day just as your perceptions do. But RPE forces you to listen to your body, which is a great lesson. Warmups and cooldowns should be between 10 and 12, and your workouts should be in the 13 to 16 range.

The walk–talk test. This is the simplest tool of the three. If you are mall walking with a friend and the conversations are as effortless as they were when you were talking over lunch, you should pick up the pace. Walk briskly enough so that when you talk, you find it a bit difficult and breathe deeply between sentences. Conversely, if you are out of breath and cannot talk and walk, slow down a bit—your intensity is too high.

Keeping a Food Diary

My friend once told me a story of a guy she went with on a camping trip. If you've ever been on one of these kinds of trips, you know how chaotic your backpack can become after days of pulling items out and stuffing them back in during low-energy, sometimes rainy times. This guy on the trip made it a point to periodically pull everything out of his pack, take stock, and then carefully repack. He said the sorting and reorganizing centered him.

That's how I feel about writing. Sometimes my head is like a backpack, needing to be emptied and reorganized so that I can take stock and become centered. Many writers say they really don't know what they think about a topic until they write about it. I agree. Getting thoughts out of your head and onto paper gives you distance and clarity.

When it comes to weight management, writing not only gives distance and clarity, it also encourages record keeping. When you keep a food diary and look back at your writing, you start to get a sense of your own eating habits. Knowing exactly what you've eaten can give you a sense of control over what can sometimes feel uncontrollable—your appetite. Keeping a food journal may even unearth an eating pattern that you had no idea about, which is excellent progress—you can't make the changes you need to make without knowing what needs to change!

(continued on page 106)

Tom's Loss Got Him Walking

I first spotted Tom on a subzero January day while I was walking with a friend at Mall of America. My friend and I saw ourselves as two big-time walkers who were stepping out at a brisk pace. We were cruising along when—*whoosh*—someone passed. His muscled arms were pumping, and his legs were blurring.

I *had* to find out who this guy was. I wanted to know how he got so fast, but even more, I wanted to know what was driving him. When our walk came to a close, I turned on my heels and headed off in hot pursuit of the walking blur. I walked in the opposite direction in the rectangular mall, hoping to cross his path.

It wasn't long before I saw him approach. He was wearing headphones, and I noticed a grin on his broad, friendly face. He was enjoying himself, I thought. He even looked a bit smug about his terrific speed. I spun and started walking his direction, gathering enough speed to match his pace.

He caught me in a snap. We were off, neck and neck. "So, do you come here often?" I asked, puffing.

"Oh yeah, now I do, just about every day," he said. I was relieved that he was also puffing.

I quickly decided to come to the point; at this speed, idle conversation is not very idle. I told him I was in the walking business, and that I looked for ways to get people off their butts and into exercise.

He glanced at me, surprised. I asked if he has always been so fit.

"Last year at this time," he said with a chuckle, "I weighed 97 pounds more than I do right now."

As we motored along, I tried to imagine this attractive, toned athlete as a 275-pound man. "How did you lose that much weight? What's your secret?"

He slowed a bit. "One year ago I lost Larry, my best friend," he said. "He died of a heart attack. He was married and had four children. And he was the same age as me."

Tom and Larry had played racquetball every Wednesday after work. "We considered ourselves to be quite the jocks," Tom said. "We always played hard. One day Larry was strutting back to the service line after a great shot. He'd been smiling, wiping the sweat off his face with his sweatband. At one point, I looked behind me at some people walking past the court. And then I heard Larry hit the floor."

Larry had a massive heart attack.

The event shocked Tom. We all have defining moments in our lives—Instants when we change, knowing we will never go back to the way we were. This was Tom's defining moment. He knew he could have been the one who died.

After Larry's death, Tom went to his doctor for a complete exam, hoping for some reassurance that what had happened to Larry would not happen to him. The visit didn't quite go the way Tom had hoped. The doctor reprimanded Tom about his excess weight, high blood pressure, and high cholesterol.

Tom's defense—that he played racquetball, ran occasionally, and was generally quite active—didn't impress the doc. "Knock off the weekend warrior stuff," his doctor ordered. "Cut the fat out of your diet. Walk every day. Lose weight. Get serious about your health."

From that point on, Tom never lacked motivation. He wisely established a plan that would work for him. "I knew the first step was to set a goal for myself," Tom said. "Right away, I decided to lose 100 pounds in a year. I knew a realistic way to meet that goal would be to lose about 2 pounds each week of the year."

Walking year-round in Minnesota is a challenge. Winter temperatures can easily dip to 20 below zero, and summertime temperatures often exceed 90 muggy degrees. So, Tom walked through 5 miles of climate-controlled skyways that enclose offices, shops, and restaurants in downtown Minneapolis, where he worked. Tom went to the office an hour early each day to walk those skyways. He lost 97 pounds in a year. While he said it was not quite the 100 pounds he was striving for, he was close enough to be proud and grateful to be alive.

Your first step is to buy a diary. It can be a slick looking one or simply a notebook, but the important factor is the size. Choose one small enough to carry with you everywhere you go.

Your assignment this week is simple: Try to record everything you eat, the portion size, the calories, and any thoughts or feelings that you associate with your eating. Do this immediately after each meal and snack. Recording immediately has two pluses: You won't forget what you ate, and you may not want to eat that snack knowing you will have to take the time to pull out the food diary and write it down. Here are a few food diary pointers.

Watch portion sizes. Check labels carefully. A careful read of the label may show that frozen macaroni and cheese entrée, for example, actually contains two servings! Getting the hang of estimating portion sizes can be difficult, especially when eating out. Yale University's Kelly Brownell, Ph.D., watched people estimate the quantities and calories in common food and beverages, such as milk, green beans, meat, and soda. On average, they were off by 60 percent! That's why Dr. Brownell recommends using a food scale. I think this is a great idea.

Condiments count, too. People often forget about the condiments or pats of butter added to foods. Don't overlook them. Those calories count and add up quickly.

Count calories. You can find the number of calories in foods in many ways. Most foods today have nutrition information right on the label. Restaurants often provide nutrition info or make it available on their Web sites. For foods without labels, such as fruits and vegetables, check out one of the many calorie-counting guides available at bookstores or online.

Note your emotions. Along with what you eat, how much, and how many calories it contains, write down how you felt while you ate. While eating lunch at a sub shop with friends, were you happy? Rushed? As you ate popcorn on the couch watching *ER*, did you feel relaxed? Stressed? Write it down.

After tracking your feelings for a few days and linking them with the food you've eaten, you'll see patterns start to emerge. You may notice you eat more when you're stressed, angry, or bored. Then you can brainstorm *other* ways to deal with these emotions, rather than looking for the solution at the bottom of the Cracker Jack box.

Remember, don't feel pressure to change anything about your eating this week—this week is all about easy starts. In weeks to come, your food diary will become a powerful tool in your weight management program. It will be your companion, confidante, and personal coach as you go through my program, so get used to carrying the diary and using it.

Behold the Calorie

Everyone who goes through a weight management program tosses around the term "calorie," but few people really know what a calorie is. I want you to know from this moment forward.

The calorie is a unit of energy. When you eat, your body receives energy from the calories in the food, and when you exercise, your body burns these calories for fuel. Did you ever wonder how scientists determine how many calories are in foods? They actually measure the calories by burning food in what is called a bomb calorimeter.

First, they dry the food, to remove the water. Then they place the food in a special container. When scientists burn the food, heat is transferred to another container full of water. Scientists define 1 calorie as the energy required to raise the temperature of 1 gram of water 1 degree centigrade. When a food such as pizza burns, it heats a lot of water and therefore has a lot of calories, compared with something like celery that heats little water.

File this information under "T" for trivia, if you wish. But the next time you are at an office party, wondering which appetizer has fewest calories, imagine dehydrating the appetizers and setting them on fire. The one that you'd guess to be the worst at heating up water is the one with the fewest calories. Maybe imagining the appetizer on fire will distract you from eating it!

Remember the Water

I talked about water in chapter 2, but because of all the good it does for us, I'd love to talk about this every day! You should drink about 4 cups of water for every 1,000 calories you eat. For most adults, that's about 10 cups (2½ quarts) of water each day. Most people do not drink enough, perhaps because we don't give it much thought. To keep it a priority, devote a section of your diary to recording how much water you drink. Simply make a check mark for every cup you drink, and tally them up at the end of the day.

People trying to manage their weight often overlook drinking water because they think water doesn't count. It has no calories and does not provide any of the other nutrients, so why bother keeping track? Water does count, even if not in the calorie column. Remember, this program is about good nutrition—not just about calories—and water is basic to good nutrition and good health. Scientists estimate that a person can lose up to 40 percent of body weight in fats, carbohydrates, and proteins and still survive. However, a 20 percent loss in body water can kill you.

An oddity about the body is that the thirst mechanism, which controls water intake, does not do the best job in keeping up with the body's need for water. If only we were more like burros. I read of one study of a burro that, after walking 8 hours in the desert, lost about 40 pounds of water, or about 5 gallons. Scientists placed the burro on a freight scale next to a watering trough. The burro drank continuously for 5 minutes, until it had replaced all of its water losses. But a human who sweats away 3 to 4 quarts (6 to 8 pounds) of body water experiences a temporary thirst that is satisfied after drinking only a pint of fluid. At that rate, it would take the person's thirst about 12 to 24 hours to "figure out" that the body is down 3 to 4 quarts, and water needs to be consumed.

Your diary will help do what your thirst mechanism will not. Each time you make a point of recording water consumption, you keep abreast of how much you have drunk and still need to drink, and you remind yourself that water is important—too important to leave to a sip here and a gulp there.

You can also use your diary to increase your water intake. You can, for instance, make a note to remind yourself to start your day with a 12- to 20-ounce eye opener, even before your coffee or tea or juice. Also try carrying a bottle filled with water all day. Make a goal to drink it before lunchtime, then fill it and drink it again before leaving work. When buying sugar-free drinks, like unsweetened iced tea, buy 20- or 32-ounce bottles of drinks, versus the 12-ounce containers. Keep a full bottle of water in your car or on your bike, and drink it before you reach your destination.

Whenever you come up with a great way to get your 10 cups, write it down in your diary so you won't forget it. As you make your way through the 8 weeks, keep a running list of all the new ways that you're devising to meet your goals. Not only do they represent a treasure trove for you, they'll also come in handy when you recruit your friends and family to mimic your success!

Thought for Week 1

From the outside, you may not feel like you've achieved that much this week—you haven't yet lost any weight, and your mall workouts may have been quite limited. But your outside cannot communicate the revolution that's begun within—you're well on your way to becoming healthier and happier.
"Well begun is half done."—Horace

5

Week 2: Lose Just 1 Pound

ow does it feel to be doing what you've wanted to do for a long time? You've officially started a mall walking and weight management program— aren't you proud of yourself? I remember being puffed up with pride when I started my second week of walking. Coming off my first week, I knew I was "in the game," part of the exercise scene that I thought would always elude me. I hope you feel the same way.

GOALS FOR WEEK 2:

- Mall walk three times, 15 minutes each

- Lose 1 pound

I also remember in those first few weeks I started noticing newspaper articles about the benefits of fitness. I'm sure they had been there all along, but I had passed over them because they didn't apply to me. However, after I started walking, they all seemed to apply to me and to be good news.

I read with great satisfaction that obese people who exercise have half the death rate of trim people who don't exercise. Then I read that walking for at least an hour a week could reduce the risk of heart disease in women, no matter how fast they walk. The risk was lowered most in women who walked with the most intensity, but it was still good to read that walking need not be fast paced in order to reap significant benefits.

Other articles explained how walking helps the head. A study of depressed people found that when people walked briskly for 30 minutes three times a week, they had sharper memories and improved ability to plan, organize, and juggle mental tasks.

Now that you exercise, you may be noticing these same kinds of articles. Clip them and put them in a file marked: "REASONS TO KEEP MALL WALKING." Look to them on those days when you feel like your get-up-and-go has got up and went.

Well on Your Way

A good start in your first week sets the stage for a successful second week. When I started walking, Jon Buzzard, athletic director at the St. Paul Athletic Club, told me to begin with walking 3 days the first week, and then plan not to miss those 3 days in the weeks that followed. If you do miss those minimum 3 days a week, he said, you begin to lose the fitness you've gained. That advice has stuck with me to this day—that's why I'm recommending you stick with your 3 mall walks, and just extend them to at least 15 minutes each.

Some of you may look at the goals for Week 2 and wonder if you're *really* exercising, or if you're taking it too easy on yourself. Maybe you think that these gentle first 2 weeks are a bit of a waste of time. My response is that I want all mall walkers to experience success while beginning. Too many exercisers start too fast too soon and end up burned out or injured 6 weeks later. I don't want that for you. I can live with a complaint that this program is too easy at the start as long as people keep coming back for more success.

(A word to exercisers who are already reasonably fit: If you *must*, go ahead and skip these 2 weeks, but I ask you to humor me here. I firmly believe that you'll gain an appreciation of mall walking and weight management by going slowly initially. Just because it isn't killing you doesn't mean it's not working—these 2 weeks give you a chance to have a successful experience with what can be a difficult change process.)

Your Calorie Needs

The second part of your mall walking goal this week is to lose 1 pound. While we could talk about a million ways to lose weight, the simple truth is that 1 pound equals 3,500 calories, so your job is to figure out how to make changes this week to burn off 3,500 more calories than you eat. You can accomplish this one of three ways:

- Eat 500 calories less each day than the number of calories you need for normal daily activities (500 calories $\times$ 7 days in a week = 3,500).

- Burn 500 calories through mall walking each day.

- Do a combination of the two, such as eating 250 calories less and mall walking 250 calories more.

The WalkSport Fit Forever Program is all about the third option, combining mall walking and eating changes to reach your desired weight. As you can see, this will require some calorie counting. Let's estimate of the number of calories you need for normal daily activities to maintain body weight. This simple formula will give you a rough estimate: Multiply your weight by 13 if you are sedentary and 15 if you are moderately active. Since you are moderately active now with mall walking, use 15.

This gives you the number of calories you need for normal daily activities, or what I call your baseline. Again, this is just a rough estimate—individual estimates vary according to your metabolism. (As you go through the process of losing weight, you may want to add or subtract 200 to 300 calories from your total if you feel that your rough estimate is wrong. A registered dietitian can offer you a more exact, professional estimate of your baseline.)

Now that you know your baseline, to lose a pound a week, shoot for a deficit of 500 calories from that number. You'll shoot for eating 250 calories per day less and mall walking 250 calories per day more. The split can be 275/225 or 300/200—whatever way you want to get to 500 calo-

Barb Cut Out Fat and Lost Weight

Calorie counting and calculating baselines may be overwhelming to you at first. If you find it difficult, keep Barb in mind. Counting calories was the last thing on her mind when she discovered she had congenital heart failure related to a viral infection. Doctors said she may need a heart transplant, but they wanted to try medication first. That helped, but her doctors also recommended that she start walking. So she headed to a nearby mall and walked, for 15 minutes a day, every day. Each week she increased her walking time by 5 minutes until she had reached 45 minutes per walk.

At that point, Barb started feeling chest pains and fatigue. Unsure as to why, she thought she may have overdone it, so she felt it would be best to lay off for a while.

That layoff lasted a year, and she became depressed, went on antidepressants, and gained 40 pounds. "I was so depressed that year, I remember watching my husband spill a can of beer," Barb says. "The beer ran across the kitchen table and onto the floor. Usually, I would have jumped up to clean the mess, but that time I just sat there and did nothing."

After what she described as the "worst winter of my life," Barb, with her doctor's approval, decided to chuck the antidepressants and start mall walking again. Slowly she began to rebuild her strength "The more I walked, the more I thought, 'I can do this,'" she says. "And that's the thing about mall walking. It is a really good exercise because I can do it and not get too tired from it."

Barb now walks 4 miles in an hour every day. She says she is cured of her depression, and there is no longer talk of a heart transplant. Oh, that 40 pounds she gained? She's walked it off, with 5 pounds to spare. She didn't do a lot of calorie counting, but she says she made two important changes in her eating: She began watching the number of grams of fat she ate, and she started serving herself smaller portions.

ries per day. After doing this for 7 days, give or take a little, you will have lost 1 pound.

In a moment, we'll talk about how to trim calories from your diet by painlessly reducing fat. But first, here's how to figure how many calories you burn mall walking: Find your weight in kilograms by dividing your weight in pounds by 2.2. Then multiply that by 3 if you walk at a slow pace (2.5 miles per hour), by 3.3 if you walk at a moderate pace (3 miles per hour), by 3.8 if you walk at a brisk pace (3.5 miles per hour), and by 5 if you walk at a very brisk pace (4 miles per hour). That result tells you how many calories you burn each hour.

So, if you weigh 150 pounds, that's 68 kilograms (150 divided by 2.2). If you walk at a brisk pace for an hour, you burn 258 calories each hour. At this rate, if you wanted to burn 500 calories each day by walking, you'd have to walk about 2 hours each day! You can see why watching calories is so important. A combination of the two makes your calorie cutting less restrictive and your mall walking less time-consuming.

Find the Fat

The fastest way to lose 1 pound this week is to determine where the fat is in your diet and reduce the amount you eat. You'll remember from earlier in the book that fat is especially calorie filled. This is especially important in these first few weeks. Since you are not mall walking daily, there are going to be days when a workout won't contribute to your 500. On the off days, try to work in more activity, but cutting fat can help get you there quicker. Here are 10 ways to reduce your fat intake.

1. **Pick picky friends.** Make friends with people who care about their fat intake and their health, and make a point of eating with them.

2. **Use fat-free yogurt instead of sour cream.** It has the same creamy texture with less fat. Use it on potatoes and in sauces, dips, and dressings. Similarly, use low-fat or fat-free dairy products.

3. **Reduce the amounts of butter in sauces and sautés** by using low-sodium chicken or vegetable broth instead. Replace the butter you put on your toast or pancakes each morning with fruit-only jam, honey, or syrup.

4. **Remove poultry skin** to reduce fat content by three-quarters and calories by half.

5. **Spice it up.** Fat is flavorful, but so are garlic, onion, ginger, basil, cilantro, rosemary, tarragon, sage, and dill.

6. **When you purchase cheese, get the best quality.** It's more flavorful, so a little bit goes a long way.

7. **Make your own pizza.** Commercial pizzas are usually loaded with high-fat cheeses and meats. But when you make your own, you'll be amazed at how tasty the pie is with a fraction (or none of) the cheese and meats.

PENCIL TIME

Reduce Your Fat Intake

Now it's your turn. I gave you 10 ideas to reduce the fat in your diet. Come up with five more.

1. _____

2. _____

3. _____

4. _____

5. _____

8. **Fix fruit dressings.** Orange, pineapple, and apple juices are a tasty substitute for oil in homemade salad dressings.

9. **Select special sauce wisely**. Many sauces on normally healthy items—like tartar sauce on fish or sour cream on burritos—contain lots of fat. Opt instead for tomato-based condiments, like cocktail sauce or salsa.

10. **Translate menus.** Restaurant menus have fancy names for fatty foods. Avoid foods that are Alfredo, Bearnaise, and tempura. Stick with steamed, baked, or broiled.

Cut Down, Not Out

I have always felt that the downfall of diets is deprivation. When I was dieting, my determination could only last so long, and then I demanded cookies. After all, what is life without cookies?

I think many people who have trouble managing their weight are constantly restraining what they eat. Not only is that just a downright unpleasant way to live, it also sets you up for failure. In one study, researchers gave restrained eaters a large milkshake or nothing before giving them a taste test. For the test, they gave both groups a large bowl of ice cream and permission to eat as much as they wanted. The restrained eaters who had a milkshake before taking the test ate much more ice cream than those who had nothing. They weren't full from the milkshake, but rather the milkshake seemed to "break" their will and cause them to go "off the wagon."

This plan is not about deprivation. Restraining is for horses chomping at the bit, not you sitting at the dinner table. I want you to have whatever you wish; just pay attention to your portions. Here's how.

Try dinky dishes. Use a luncheon-size plate for dinner so that you have to be careful with your portion sizes. Using smaller plates, bowls, and glasses makes sensible portions look larger.

Slow down. The message of satiety takes about 20 minutes to move from stomach to brain. Eating slower will make a sensible portion seem bigger and give your body time to feel satisfied.

Think seconds. You can always go back for additional sensible portions. But chances are you won't. Most people are conditioned to feel finished when their plate is clean.

Buy the smaller bag. A study at the University of Illinois found that when customers were given larger snack containers, they ate an average of 44 percent more popcorn and 40 percent more M&Ms. That added up to 40 to 50 percent more calories. Larger containers can be a better value, but smaller bags may make you cherish each bite more and slow your eating to make the bag last longer.

Repackage. If you just can't resist the economy-size package, split it into small portions in plastic bags or containers for later use.

Close the bag. When eating super tempting foods like chips (betcha can't eat just one!), put just one serving on a plate, then seal the bag and put it away. This will remove the temptation to eat more. And when you see how little you really get for such a huge number of fat grams, it may be enough to put you off chips for good!

Be size wise. Fast food restaurants' splashy ads urge us to buy the super-size meals. Trouble is that those meals clock in at close to the 2,000

PENCIL TIME

Pay Attention to Portions

Again, it's your turn. In the space below, write five additional ways to limit the size of your portions while eating out or at home.

1. _____

2. _____

3. _____

4. _____

5. _____

calories a day the average adult needs. Ignore the ads and meal deals—they will still take your money if you just order a simple hamburger and a small Coke.

Bag the bread. When dining out and the basket of great-tasting bread comes to your table, eat one slice and ask the waitress if you can take the remaining slices home in a bag. Enjoy your meal, and then eat the bread with fruit the next day.

Go half and half. Eat half of your entrée and enjoy a salad and extra vegetables with it. Take home the remaining half of the entrée to eat the next day, and ease your cooking load for a second night.

Order an appetizer as your entrée. If you are hungry, order two healthy appetizers such as a bowl of hearty bean soup and a garden salad instead of an appetizer *plus* a rich meal.

Avoid alcohol. Nothing like getting "happy" to make you order more than you had intended to eat.

Take take-out out. Instead of eating out of the container, scoop it out and serve it on a plate so you can see how large the servings are. Also, eating from a compact box can seem like you're eating a snack, not a meal, making you more likely to overeat.

Thought for Week 2

A good serving of humor serves you well as you finish Week 2 and continue with the WalkSport Fit Forever Program. If you feel yourself becoming a bit too serious this week about your portion sizes, counting calories, and cutting back on fats, then remember Redd Foxx, who said: "Health nuts are going to feel stupid someday, lying in the hospital dying of nothing." Moderation is the key—don't go "nutty!"

6

Week 3: Let's Power Walk!

Every morning, 7 days a week, Elaine is up-and-at-'em doing her mall walks. She's been doing it faithfully for the past 9 years with great results.

"I like the morning light that comes into the mall. I especially like the camaraderie. I can always find someone to walk with, who is not going too fast or too slow," she says.

Before "Every Morning Elaine" goes to the mall, she does a variety of stretches. "After I stretch, I have a better stride and rhythm when I walk," she says. Then she drives to the mall and walks slowly for the first 3 to 4 minutes.

I definitely give Elaine high marks for warming up before her morning walks. But like many exercisers, Elaine is out of order with her pre-walking routine. She stretches then warms up when she should be warming up, *then* stretching. This becomes especially important to you this week.

Up until this week, your mall walking workouts have been easy enough for you to be successful but not too hard on your body. Now we're going to

GOALS FOR WEEK 3:

• Mall walk four times, 20 minutes each time

• Make one of your four walks a Power Walk

• Lose 1 pound

• Create a weekly food plan

(continued on page 124)

WalkSport Fit Forever Stretching Routine

Go to a place in your mall near a bench and a wall. It's time to stretch.

Calf Stretch

Take a big step forward with your left foot, bending your left knee. Keep your right leg straight and your bent knee directly above your foot. If this causes pain, move your feet closer together. Move your hips forward, keeping both feet pointing forward and your right heel on the floor. Feel the stretch in your right calf. Repeat with your right foot forward.

Hamstring Stretch

Stand about 2 feet away from a bench. Place your right leg on the bench. Bend your left leg slightly. With your hands on your right thigh, bend forward at the waist. Don't hunch your back or press down on your thigh. Feel the stretch in the back of your right leg, the hamstring area. Repeat for the left leg.

Quadriceps Stretch

Stand with your left hand against a wall or bench for balance. Bend your right leg and grab your right foot or ankle behind you. Gently pull your foot toward your buttocks. Keep your knees together and your hips square and forward. Feel the stretch in the front of your right leg. Repeat with your left leg.

Hip and Thigh Stretch

Stand sideways to a wall and place your left palm on the wall for support. Cross your right leg over your left leg and push your left hip toward the wall. Keep your left leg straight and allow your right to bend. Feel the stretch in your left hip. Repeat on the other side.

Shin Stretch

Face a wall, standing about an arm's length away. Using your arms for support, bend your knees forward and roll your right foot forward until the top of the foot faces downward and the sole is up. Bend your knees a little more to feel the stretch in your right shin. Repeat on the opposite side.

Back Stretch

Stand sideways to a wall, about 18 inches away. Turn toward the wall and put both palms on the wall at chest level. Gently keep turning toward the wall. Repeat in the opposite direction.

(continued)

Chest Stretch

Stand with feet shoulder-width apart and your back to a wall. Reach back and place one of your palms on the wall, with your wrist facing out and your arm straight. Gently turn your head and chest away from the wall. You will feel the stretching in the chest and in the front of the shoulders as well. Repeat on the other side.

Shoulder Stretch

Stand with feet shoulder-width apart and knees slightly bent. Raise your right arm to shoulder height. Grasp your right elbow with your left hand and pull your right arm across your body. Move your shoulder up and down to feel the stretch in different areas of the shoulder. Repeat with your left arm.

Hip and Buttock Stretch

Sit on the floor with your legs extended forward. Cross your left foot over to the outside of your right knee. Now bring your right arm across your body and press your right elbow against your left knee. Turn your head and shoulders to the left. Feel the stretch in your right hip and buttock. It feels great on the back as well. Repeat with the other leg.

Groin Stretch

Sit on the floor, knees bent and soles of your feet together. Bring your feet in, as close to your body as is comfortable. Grab your ankles and lean forward, making sure you keep your spine straight.

Lower Back Stretch

Lie flat on your back. Pull your knees toward your chest until your hips come off the floor. Hold the stretch and then extend your legs slowly, one at a time.

start picking up the pace, moving to four 20-minute workouts. To kick us off, I'll talk about components of a serious workout and introduce you to power walking. You'll also learn how to make a weekly food plan.

Workout Components

Every good, serious workout should boast four distinct components: warmup, stretch, workout, and cooldown. Each of these is an important part of building and maintaining fitness and protecting yourself from injury, beginning with the essential warmup.

Warmup. To warm up, set out walking for 5 minutes, beginning slowly and gradually increasing your speed until you feel your body temperature is above normal. It's important to warm up before working out, because warm muscles are more efficient than cold muscles. When the temperature is elevated, muscle enzymes work better, nerve impulses travel faster for improved coordination, and increased blood flow means better delivery of fuel for energy. Warmed muscle tissue is also more pliable, and tendons and ligaments are less prone to injury.

An adequate warmup also helps your heart prepare for aerobic exercise and allows your mind to inventory any aches that need to be worked out, helping you transition into your workout. The warmup should be a slight rehearsal for the main event, your mall walking workout.

Stretch. Researchers say that for moderate activities like mall walking, stretching right after warming up is optional. They say you can concentrate on stretching after the walk is over because then muscles are really warm and the stretching is more beneficial.

I like to recommend doing both, some light stretches before and then deep stretches after a workout. I think we can learn from Elaine, who said stretching beforehand allows her to have a better stride and rhythm when she walks. After warming up, do each of the stretches on pages 120 to 123 for 10 seconds, stretching to the point of tension, not pain. Don't bounce or bob, and breathe naturally while you stretch. If you are a little embarrassed to be stretching in a mall, find an out-of-the-way corner or hallway to stretch in, or schedule your workout early in the morning.

Workout. During the workout section, you'll simply mall walk at your desired pace, for the full time recommended in the goals for that week. For instance, for Week 3, you would walk for 20 minutes at any pace you feel comfortable with.

Cooldown. The cooldown period is equal in time and importance to the warmup. After a good walk, if you do not wind down with slow walking and stretching, blood tends to pool in the lower half of your body. Because of lack of blood flow to the brain, this can lead to a sudden drop in blood pressure, dizziness, or even fainting. Cooldowns also help minimize muscle soreness and fatigue.

To cool down, walk at an easy pace for 5 minutes. Monitor your pulse two or three times in a minute, until it is back down close to your normal. In a 6-year study at the Cleveland Clinic in Ohio, cardiologists found that how quickly your heart rate drops after exercise is an important predictor of heart attack risk. People with slow recovery rates were four times more likely to die within the 6 years of the study than people with normal recovery rates. At about the 1-minute mark following a moderately hard workout, doctors say your heart rate should drop by at least 12 beats per minute from your exercising rate. If it stays high, see your doctor.

Cooldown is also the time for deep stretching. Your muscles have been shortening and contracting forcibly during your mall walking, so it makes sense that they would benefit from stretching during cooldowns, when the muscles are at their warmest and most pliable. So repeat the above stretches, only this time hold each stretch for 30 seconds. This allows enough time for the muscle to release its initial resistance and then relax.

Make these four components a part of every basic workout, whether you're ambling along or really pushing yourself. Speaking of challenges, let's look at this week's calorie-burning secret weapon: Power Walking.

Power Walking

Becky mall walks to the beat of a different drummer. She performs as a puppeteer at schools, libraries, and churches. Her performances are high-energy, using 12 to 15 puppets per show, each with a different voice and personality.

(continued on page 128)

The WalkSport Fit Forever Power Walking Routine

Make the most of your exercise time by mixing these fun strengthening exercises into your mall walks.

1. Do easy warmup walking for about 5 minutes.

2. Stretch, as described on pages 120 to 123.

3. Walk for 3 minutes. Even though you are warmed up, go at a slow to moderate pace for the first minute or so, and then pick up the pace so you are walking in the upper end of your target heart rate zone. This is the "somewhat hard" area of the perceived exertion scale.

4. Stop walking. Find an out-of-the-way place to do your exercises, and using a wall or a railing for support, do a squat, which strengthens the quadriceps and buttocks. To do the squat, stand with feet shoulder-width apart. Slowly bend your knees and push back your hips as you lower into a squat. The angle at your knees should not exceed 90 degrees. In fact, start off with a slight squat this week and work up to deeper squats in later weeks. Hold the squat for 1 minute, making sure you breathe normally. Slowly stand and resume walking.

Step 4

Step 6

5. Walk "hard" for 3 minutes.

6. Stop walking. For 1 minute, slowly do push-ups, which strengthen the chest and arms. Position yourself on the floor so your body is straight and your weight is on your hands and feet—or hands and knees if you prefer a less strenuous pushup. Your hands should be flat on the floor and directly beneath your shoulders. Slowly lower your chest until it touches the floor. Push yourself back up, exhaling when you push. (Wall pushups are easiest—stand an arm's length from the wall, with palms flat on the wall, shoulder height, fingertips turned in slightly. Lean forward, allowing your elbows to bend and chest to touch the wall, then straighten.)

Don't race to see how many pushups you can do. Just use steady movements, using the pushups to build strength. After 1 minute, stand and walk.

7. Walk "hard" for 3 minutes.

Step 8

8. Stop and, for 1 minute, do rows, which strengthen the back and arms. Find a post at the bottom of a stairway and grasp it hand over hand. If you cannot locate a stair post, find a railing and grasp it with both hands, palms down. Stand 2 feet away from the post or railing, with feet hip-width apart. Slowly sit back and down into a squat position, arms straight. Slowly pull your chest toward the post or railing, working the biceps and back. Pull until your chin is near the post or railing, and then steadily straighten your arms until you are in the original squat position. Repeat this process slowly for 1 minute and then walk.

Step 10

9. Walk "hard" for 3 minutes.

10. Stop and, for 1 minute, do standing wall crunches, which strengthen the abdominal muscles. Stand with your back to a wall, your feet shoulder-width apart and about a foot away from the wall. Bend your knees slightly and lean your back against the wall. Contract your stomach muscles. This causes your pelvic area to curl upward and your chest to be pulled slightly downward. Feel the contraction. Release and repeat for 1 minute. Stand and walk.

11. Walk "hard" for 3 minutes.

12. Stop, and for 1 minute, do bent-over leg extensions, which strengthen lower back muscles. Stand facing a wall or railing, 2 or 3 feet away from it. Lean forward from the hips, and place your hands on the wall or railing for support. Slowly move your right leg backward and up, keeping the leg fairly straight. You should feel your back muscles pulling and some stretching in the thigh of your support leg. Your ultimate goal is to be able to move the leg far enough so that it is parallel with the ground. Slowly lower the leg to its original position and repeat for 1 minute. Make sure you do an equal number of repetitions for both right and left legs.

13. Complete the session with a 5-minute walking cooldown and then the cooldown stretches described on page 125.

Step 12

To maintain her vigor and energy, Becky incorporates Power Walking into her workouts. She goes to the out-of-the-way corners of the mall and does exercises to break up her mall walking workout. She'll hook a heel on a railing and do stretches to loosen up an old back injury. She'll do squats, lean against the wall and lift one leg at a time, and sit on a bench and raise her hands high to stretch her trunk, all in an effort to do more of a full-body workout. This week, you'll follow Becky's lead and make your fourth walk a Power Walk, mixing in strength and flexibility exercises.

Strength training was once just for Arnold Schwarzenegger types who wanted great bodies—now, it is for people who want great lives. Experts say strength training maintains or increases your muscle mass and metabolic rate, reduces body fat, increases bone mineral density, improves glucose metabolism, speeds up transit time of food through your gastrointestinal system, helps lower blood pressure and cholesterol, improves low back pain, reduces arthritic aches, and gives you a boost in confidence. Not a bad list of benefits for something that only takes a few minutes of your workout!

These Power Walk exercises were developed for WalkSport by certified personal trainer Nancy Anderson of Minneapolis. We'll start with five exercises this week, and add more in future weeks. Don't worry—you're not going to be heaving dumbbells around as you walk the mall. In your Power Walking workouts, you'll get a taste of strength training that will hopefully encourage you to look into strength training classes. (While these exercises are safe and effective, you must have your physician's approval before you do them.)

You are now ready for your first Power Walk.

A Weekly Food Plan

Your final goal for the week lets you use your food diary to develop a weekly food plan. For many people, losing weight means losing interest in food because they think they cannot have the foods they want. You *can* have what you want—just eat smaller portions and watch your fat intake. A weekly food plan will help you do this.

Most of us start the week with an activity plan in mind, if not on paper. We schedule mall walks, hair appointments, work deadlines, place-of-worship meetings, lunch dates, car tune-ups, golf outings, kids' practices, choir rehearsals—the list goes on and on. We may even take some justifiable pride in what we can get done in a week when we plan well. But the same people who take pride in their organizational abilities may resist planning when it comes to food. Some don't like meal planning because they don't want to fall into the "it's-Monday-so-it-must-be-meat-loaf" rut they remember their parents fell into. Instead, they eat on the run, catching as catch can.

I believe that the risk of getting into a rut—a fattening rut at that—is greater when you *don't* plan than when you do. People are creatures of habit, and when we are bushed, harried, or unprepared, we often resort to the same old same old. You stagger into the kitchen after a dizzying day and gaze at the cupboards, hoping for inspiration to strike. Your stomach is rumbling, and gastric—not creative—juices are flowing.

With a weekly meal plan, you know what's for dinner, but also the portions are right, the meal is balanced, and you eat the variety of foods needed for good nutrition. Perhaps the biggest bonus is that you are not nagged by "What's for dinner?" all day.

Open your food diary and think about what kinds of meals you'll enjoy during Week 3. Here are some helpful suggestions to help you plan.

Plan your planning time. Establish a set time to plot out your meals for each week. Pick a time when you are fresh, like a weekend morning. Go to the mall, do your walk, buy a cup of coffee, and make a food plan for the next 7 days, or dictate it into your micro-cassette recorder.

Keep it simple. Write each day of the week on the next seven pages of your food diary. Each day, list the three to six foods and beverages you want for each meal. Refer to the Food Guide Pyramid to help you cover all the food groups for each day.

Watch the fat. Remember that fat harbors many calories, so build your plan around low-fat items.

Remember breakfast. Many people with weight problems skip breakfast, and then make up for it—big-time—the rest of the day. Eat well in the morning, and you will be less ravenous at later meals, which are usually made up of foods higher in fat than breakfast foods.

If the breakfast space in your weekly food plan is consistently blank, fill it in with cereals, juice, fruit, oatmeal, toast, yogurt, bagels with peanut butter or cream cheese, an occasional egg with bacon, pita bread stuffed with light cheese, and even salmon on toast with low-fat cottage cheese. If cereal is all you can manage, be sure to choose one that's high in fiber and whole grains, so you don't head out the door every day with a belly full of Fruit Loops. If you are not hungry in the morning, you may be eating too much before going to bed—which, coincidentally, is another habit of people with weight problems.

Make the most of lunch. I consider lunches to be "speed bump" meals. Just as a speed bump slows speeding autos, a lunch slows speeding humans hurtling through their hectic days. Ignoring speed bumps is hard on cars, and ignoring lunches is hard on bodies and minds. Your body needs a midday boost in energy, and your mind needs a break so you have some freshness to finish the day.

If you're not using your lunch hour to mall walk, don't work through lunch or use the time to do errands. Make lunch plans that are more elaborate than writing "Burger King." Fast food is often nothing more than a high-fat fix. Instead, plan to have more control over your lunches. Brown bagging it at least a few days means you can pack sandwiches, salads, fruit, yogurt, soups—just about anything. I have learned to double or triple my favorite recipes so that I can have intentional leftovers to quickly grab the next morning and use for lunch. I prepare these leftovers on weekends, when I have more time to cook.

Brown bagging makes for more healthy lunches because you choose nutritious foods rather than taking your chances with vending machines or fast-food restaurants. If you pack your lunch, eat away from your workplace to clear your mind and break any stress that is building in you.

Dine light. If you've done breakfast and lunch right, dinner should not be a big feast. Instead, make it a fun time to be with family and friends, a nutritious and relaxing transition from *work* time to *your* time.

When you assume that one night you will probably eat out and another you will have leftovers, all you really need is five good dinners for the week. So during your planning time, pull those dusty cookbooks from the shelf and do a search for your Fab Five. You will have five in a snap. In fact, you will probably choose 15 before you realize it, salivating to try them all.

Snack smart. Nibbling on snacks can be good for you when you think healthy. That means dry cereals, popcorn, fruits and dried fruits, low-fat muffins, frozen fruit bars, whole wheat crackers, pretzels, vegetable sticks, baked potatoes, nuts, and seeds. Healthy also means avoiding too much sugar, salt, and fat. A cookie or a handful of peanuts is okay as a snack before a meal, but you don't want these snack foods to *become* your meal.

By nature, snacks are supposed to taste really good, so take care not to overeat. Prepackage your snacks or take the amount you want out of the bag and then seal it before you start eating. When you know you have a predetermined amount of a snack available, you automatically tend to slow down your eating and savor each bite.

I especially like an afternoon snack to boost my energy for the "home stretch" of the workday. This snack, like all snacks, not only provides energy but it also curbs my appetite so I don't become carelessly hungry and overeat at dinner.

Controlling your cravings is one of the biggest bonuses of planning your meals. Along with your increased workouts and Power Walk, you'll have no problem losing your pound this week.

Thought for Week 3

If you are resisting doing your food plan this week, think about those times when you didn't plan, started grazing, and ended up pigging out. The calories really add up quickly. Which brings to mind a quote I once read: "Calories don't count; they multiply."

7

Week 4: Controlling Those Cravings

Meet Pat, your guide this week. Her example serves as a review of some of the key points we have covered so far. She will also walk you through three new topics: controlling cravings, avoiding high-risk food situations, and using good walking form.

GOALS FOR WEEK 4:

- Mall walk four times, 25 minutes each time

- Make one of your four walks a Power Walk, using 4-minute "hard" walking intervals

- Work on walking form

- Lose 1 pound

Fourteen years ago, Pat ate a bad burger and came down with *E. coli* food poisoning that developed into hemolytic uremic syndrome.

The disease suppressed Pat's immune system, and she developed severe asthma, chronic fatigue syndrome, fibromyalgia, and memory lapses. She was forced to cut back her hours as an accounting clerk for a wholesale florist. She slogged through 6 long years in this condition.

"I couldn't walk 10 feet without being exhausted," Pat says. "My washer and dryer are in the basement, and whenever I did the laundry, I stayed in the basement all day. I could hardly go up and down stairs."

Pat went through a debilitating, housebound year. "I told myself that I had to do something, that I couldn't live like this," she says.

Small Steps toward Success

The "something" that Pat did was walk. Desperately determined to change, she joined a mall walking club, thinking maybe a formal program would help her. But she was too weak to consistently make it to the mall. She tried walking in her neighborhood, but she fell down a lot because of weakness and lack of equilibrium. After one doctor visit, she tried crossing a street to a grocery store. She made it across the street but fell twice in the store parking lot. "I sat on the pavement to rest, and then picked myself up and kept going," Pat remembers.

During this time of humbling victories and considerable pain, Pat kept going. "Every day I was extremely depressed, sitting at home with the four walls closing in around me." Only her determination stopped her depression from doing her in. Pat made a goal of walking halfway around her block. When she finally made it, she sat on a neighbor's lawn to rest before heading home. Her next goal was to walk two blocks. After 5 months of setting and reaching goal after goal, Pat finally made it three-fourths of a mile to the bus stop. She took the bus to the mall, and there she sat on a bench and just rested, extremely pooped but proud.

At that point, Pat's ultimate goal had been getting to the mall. Walking outside was okay, but she discovered that outdoor allergies were sapping what little energy she had. She knew that if she fell in the mall, help was readily available. Pat also knew that, as determined as she was, she needed support and could find it at the mall. Sure enough, over the next few weeks of walking to and from the bus stop and resting at the mall, Pat met other mall walkers. "So many of them encouraged me along the way," she says. "After being cooped up for months, just to be able to sit in a mall and chit-chat was wonderful for helping me eliminate my depression. That support is key," she says.

Buoyed by her new friends, Pat made it partway around the mall and started attending mall walking club meetings. As she became stronger, her walks became longer. She started stretching and then doing strength training exercises with 1-pound weights. It wasn't long before she was a regular mall walker. She even lost 54 pounds and was named Mall Walker of the Year by her club.

Pat could be the poster child for much of what we've talked about so far. Her story touches on the importance of:

- The mall as an ideal place to walk
- The support of a mall walking community
- An optimistic, can-do attitude
- Setting small-but-attainable intermediate goals
- Treating depression with mall walking
- Stretching and strength training
- Exercise for weight loss

Almost lost in Pat's inspirational story is the pretty impressive fact that she lost 54 pounds in a year. Mall walking was a factor, but certainly not the only one. She also keeps a food diary. "I write down every morsel of food I put into my mouth," she says.

The food diary helps Pat watch what she eats, but she emphasizes that watching what she eats is different from dieting. "What I do is not a diet," she says, "it's proper eating." Part of proper eating is drinking plenty of water. She says drinking bottle after bottle of water helps her eat less food and practice good nutrition. Pat is also particular about portion sizes. Remembering to limit portion sizes has helped her avoid the deprivation thinking that can undermine weight management. "You can eat almost anything you want—just watch your portion sizes," she advises.

This week I want you to be like Pat. Use your food diary to record all that you eat and to do another weekly food plan. I also want you to write about your food cravings.

Controlling Cravings

Cravings can creep up on you. You can be going through your day in blissful harmony with the universe, when an innocent whiff of chocolate invades your space. Eleven chocolate-chip cookies later (take one more, they're small), and you are wondering what hit you.

That's not all you should be wondering. Instead of sitting among empty wrappers, shell-shocked, ask yourself several questions: Were you actually hungry or were psychological factors at play? Is this urge linked to a time of day or a place, such as passing a fast-food restaurant? Do you get this urge regularly, like during dessert time? Is the urge associated with a person or a pleasant event? Is the food more about providing comfort than satisfying hunger?

This week, when you are recording your day's eating in your food diary, begin to note any food cravings you're having, and include the answers to the questions above. Before you give in, try some of these tips to prepare you for that next chocolate-laden whiff.

Eat well. When your belly is full of healthy foods, you just don't have room for much more. So even if you do cave in to a craving, chances are the damage will be less when you've already eaten more of the good stuff.

Drink up. Same deal. If you're full of water, it will be easier to confront a food craving. Also, thirst can sometimes mimic hunger—you may think you're ravenous, but your body's just craving water.

Distract yourself. When you have a sense that a craving is stalking you, walk away from it. "When I get a craving, it's like there's a hole inside me," says Pat. "Mall walking fills that hole, because after I exercise, I don't have that craving anymore. Also, mall walking helps me take my mind off myself." You can also distract yourself with other fun activities, such as planning vacations, playing music, singing, sewing, writing letters, taking a shower, or washing the car. Usually, when you are done, the craving has passed or is not as potent.

Think portions. Pat's daughter once brought home a dozen Krispy Kreme doughnuts, Pat's favorite. "I'll have a small piece," Pat told her daughter, and she stuck to her word. By doing this, she "tossed a bone" toward her craving, keeping it calm while she savored just a little of the sweet taste. I have found after a few episodes of eating smaller portions of something sweet that I have less of a sweet tooth and, therefore, less of a craving. By the way, that kind of motherly example has helped Pat, her daughter, and her husband lose a combined 150 pounds.

Avoiding High-Risk Situations

Keeping your food diary can be an invaluable source of information to help you notice patterns and detect high-risk situations. These are the occasions, like with Pat and the doughnuts, when you got into trouble with overeating or eating poorly. It happens. However, reviewing your diary will help you spot trouble before it occurs again.

Your diary may reveal that there are times when you feel less control over your eating, such as before bedtime or on weekends. Knowledge is power, so before one of those times occurs, schedule a distracting activity. You may find that you are especially at risk when you have feelings of boredom, depression, loneliness, joy, or anger. When you start having these feelings, try distraction or staying with the feelings. Process them instead of trying to crowd them out with food.

Your high-risk situation may involve a particular person, such as one friend who has a thing for ice cream or another friend who handles work stress by eating piles of onion rings. Don't delete these people from your friends file. Just plan events with them that don't involve food, eat well before your meet with them, and be watchful so you don't follow in their wake of overeating.

Is there a room in your home that is trouble? For example, do you always head to the den with a drink and TV snack? If so, limit your eating to one room, like the dining room. Watch TV in the den but do it without food. Or watch, but learn to juggle or sew—anything but eat.

Holidays and parties can be risky because the atmosphere is festive, everyone seems to be eating and enjoying themselves, and the food is free and tasty. You may want to eat so that you are doing something versus standing there all alone. You may also have the urge to relax and celebrate—and keep eating. By all means, go to the party, but plan ahead, anticipating the food and the people you will encounter. Eat something nutritious before you go. Avoid the chips, dips, and nuts, and save your calories for two interesting and tasty dishes you normally don't eat. Eat slowly and pay attention to the nuances of the flavors.

With a little thought, you can avoid many high-risk situations. Pat makes a point of walking at the mall at 7 A.M. "Nothing is open at that time, so I can forget about eating," she says. "At that hour, I am focused on what is important." However, it is no big deal to Pat if she happens to be in the mall when the food court opens. "You really can't avoid all high-risk situations," she says. "If a friend wants to go to Burger King, I go and eat half of everything. I just plan ahead and think about portion size. And if I eat the whole thing, oh well, I fell off my horse for one day. I just get back on the next."

Using Good Walking Form

If you're getting yourself to the mall, lacing up those shoes, and spending 25 minutes walking, you may as well get the maximum bang for your time investment. Proper walking form, including the components of maintaining correct posture, finding your stride, and using your arm muscles, can help you walk more efficiently and safely, preventing injury and ensuring more walks to come.

Maintaining Correct Posture

To really have the best posture, walk "naked." If I don't have you blushing with this suggestion, at least I have your attention!

My intent with this image is to change your posture and increase the effectiveness of your walking. Good form can make mall walking easier on your body and more fun. I helped Pat with her form. "I was slouching too much," Pat says. "So I straightened up, tucked my butt in a bit, and got my arms more involved in my striding. This all helped me increase my pace, which made me breathe harder, which eased my asthma."

Often I speak to groups on the benefits of fitness walking, or teach classes on walking techniques to people like Pat. When I comment on adjusting posture to improve walking workout, I suddenly see everyone in the audience grow an inch all at once. The room fills with taller, more powerful-looking people.

Most of us want improved posture and know it's good for us. Yet often we don't think about this critical factor. That's understandable, since it's hard to evaluate our posture unless we're standing in front of a mirror.

Once we become conscious of posture, though, we do pretty well. The suggestion to walk "naked" helps us become conscious of posture. The phrase elicits action from us because we can tie the idea to a startling sensation—the feeling of being naked and wanting to look good. When I tell mall walkers to walk "naked," their posture immediately improves, tucking in their tummies, throwing back their shoulders, and straightening their backs. Their chins level out, and they move their heads so that their ears are in line with their shoulders and hipbones.

These adjustments can make an enormous difference in toning abdominal muscles. When you take strides with good posture, you work your abdominal muscles more. That's good news if you want a flatter stomach. Looks aside, weakened abdominal muscles paired with a flabby tummy put a nasty strain on the lower back.

Try these good-posture suggestions right now.

- Stand and imagine that you are about to walk naked.
- Position your hips over your knees and feet.
- Place your shoulders over your hips. Some people need to consciously feel as though they are tucking their hips in and directly beneath their shoulders.
- Make sure your head is directly over your shoulders, not angled forward.

This may feel a bit awkward, but you will become comfortable with this position in time. When I teach my classes, I help people line up their body so they are in good posture. In this position, some people feel as though they are going to tip over backward. They are not tipping, but it feels that different to them. If this good-posture position causes you to feel as if you are tipping backward, have a friend give you the once-over. Ask if you are leaning, hunching, or lurching forward when you walk. If so, ask them to help you into a good-posture position. Memorize how you feel in this position, which will feel normal in no time.

If you're having trouble achieving this posture, another way might be better for you. Try this alternative method of adjusting your posture. (Again, try this while standing.)

- Place your feet shoulder-width apart.

- Let your arms relax and fall at your side. Also, allow your shoulders to relax.

- Keep your chin level.

- Take a big, deep breath, filling your chest with air.

- Hold your breath briefly. Then let it go, keeping your chest in position as if it were still filled with air.

Now that's good posture! Notice that your hips and ribs are not scrunched together like they are when you slouch. You have all that room to breathe, and your upper body is lifted. You are probably standing an inch or so taller and look 5 pounds lighter. You might feel a bit of strain at first, but this is a friendly strain on muscles that will eventually strengthen and support the great posture of your back. The posture of your back is especially important when you are trying to gain walking speed, which you will continue to do as your mall walking progresses. We all have a natural tendency to tilt forward from the waist or neck as we walk faster. Avoid this tilting and you will avoid a sore back from mall walking.

Walking with good posture might feel tiresome and take considerable concentration in the beginning. But in a little time, your abdomen will firm up and this new posture will become natural. The next time you mall walk, use your imagination. Picture yourself walking tall, strong—and naked!

Finding Your Stride

Walkers often get carried away with stride length when they walk fast. They unnaturally lengthen their stride, taking big, "giraffe" steps. These people reason that to go faster, they just need to take longer strides. At one time I thought the same way. Tall people who have longer legs can go faster, right?

Wrong. This misconception can actually interfere with walking efficiency. People who have set race-walking records have been relatively short in stature. The reason: Skilled race walkers always have their feet in contact with the surface they're walking on, and doing this is more efficient when strides are shorter—not longer.

Walking requires a repetitive push-and-pull. Time and again, you push off the back leg and pull with your lead leg. For example, your left arm swings forward as your left leg pushes backward; at the same time, your right arm swings backward as the right leg pulls the body forward. The more push-and-pull you do, the faster you go, the more muscles you work, and the more calories you burn. Shortening your stride moves your feet faster, which promotes this push-and-pull and increases your speed. Shortening also minimizes the inefficient jolting motion that you can see when someone walks with long, loping steps.

Here's another important benefit of shortening your stride: It shortens the "brake phase" of each step. When your heel strikes the ground in front of you, you brake, causing a momentary slowing of your stride. This braking is jarring and a waste of energy; first you generate forward speed when you push off with a rear foot, only to immediately lose some of that speed when your front foot "pole vaults" into the floor in front of you. You can minimize braking by shortening your stride so that your heel lands more directly underneath your nose. In this way, your foot is rolling through the braking process and quickly preparing for propulsion.

As you stride, don't lock your knees or hyperextend them forcefully. This can damage your joints and the tissues in and around them. You don't want to feel your knee joint snapping backward. Your knee should feel firm, but not rigid.

While it may take some time to perfect, it really pays to find your stride. You'll experience better and more enjoyable workouts. Let me offer this stride guide: First, experiment with different stride lengths. Warm up for about 10 minutes, making sure your muscles are loose, then for 30 yards or so take strides that are unusually long for you. Feel the excess bounce? Then for another 30 yards take strides that are unusually short for you. Feel the lack of flow and power? You may even want to alternate between really long and really short strides to get a firm idea of what stride length you don't want. Finally, find a stride length in between, one that has flow and power and comfort to it. Memorize what this stride feels like. You may also want to ask a friend to watch you experiment with strides, so that she can tell you how you look when you finally find *your* stride.

Using Your Arms

Most of us think of walking as working the legs but, for the most part, not the arms. By contrast, swimming and cross-country skiing are excellent activities for gaining overall muscle strength as well as aerobic conditioning. Both are wonderful, low-impact sports. Unfortunately, many people find these sports to be neither as convenient nor as accessible as walking. Often there's no snow or no pool when and where you want to work out.

Enter NordicTrack and other companies that created exercise machines to simulate cross-country skiing. These machines capitalize on the concept of the "whole-body workout." Many of them work beautifully and can be stored for easy use in your bedroom or basement, provided you have the space.

But there's a hitch: To use these machines, you're confined to your basement or bedroom, where the scenery is limited to hot water heaters or unmade beds. Also, you're not likely to take your machine on the road during a business trip or a vacation.

So how can you get the most upper body exercise from your workouts? The strengthening exercises of your Power Walks have shown you that mall walking can be a whole-body workout. But the power swinging of your arms while you mall walk can also contribute to a whole-body workout. By using a specific arm swing, you can work your arms harder than in normal walking.

Power swinging basically entails walking with your arms at a 90-degree angle. You may find it takes a little time to get used to this, but if you don't mind looking a bit "different," you'll find the technique well worth the change. It works the arms, builds muscle, helps you walk faster, and puts less strain on your lower back.

To get your arms into the act, take the following steps:

- Stand straight and face a mirror. Let your arms relax at your sides with your hands in soft fists. (If you clench your fists tightly, you tend to tense up your whole body.) Relax your shoulders.

- Bring your fists up, bending your elbows into 90-degree angles. I call this the power-arm position.

- Start swinging your power arms. Keep facing the mirror and notice whether your shoulders start to tighten and sneak upward. If so, relax and let them come down. Swing your power arms back far enough to feel a tug in the muscles of your chest and your arms, and a contraction of the upper back, shoulder, and triceps muscles. (You may need to focus on these sensations awhile.) Swinging the arms in this range of motion will tone and build muscles.

- Keep your thumbs tucked in. If you make fists with your thumbs sticking up like a hitchhiker, you can snag them on a pocket, which is annoying and can hurt.

- Continuing to swing your power arms, turn sideways and look in the mirror. Are your arms maintaining their 90-degree angles?

- Don't swing your arms too far forward, which can cause a swagger and an unnecessary strain in your lower back. When swinging the arms back, stop your fists at the hipbone. When swinging forward, stop the fists at nipple level.

- No "chicken-winging." Make sure your arms swing close to your body and you are pulling your elbows straight back.

- Don't "body punch" with your arms, swinging them across your body, as if you were body punching a bad guy. Keep your walks friendly and your power arms swinging at your sides.

You may feel pretty good about yourself as you stand in front of the mirror, power arms swinging in perfect cadence and in the right range of motion. Now let's take this new power-arm form for a test run.

Start walking in your normal stride, using a hands-lowered arm swing.

As you continue to walk, gradually raise your arms to the power-arm position. Swing the arms in cadence and in the right range of motion. I have found that beginners may think too hard about this new arm swing, and their natural arm-leg coordination is thrown off. If that happens to you, drop your arms and walk normally. From time to time, try raising your arms to the power position briefly. You will get it. I have seen countless people befuddled by this for just a bit and then, bingo, they get it—and a big smile to go with it!

You can also try the power-arm swinging for one lap, and then relax for a lap. Also, when doing the power-arm laps, try thinking about only one aspect of the technique at a time. For instance, for one lap concentrate only on your shoulders staying down. Relax your arms for a mindless lap, and then do another power-arm lap, thinking only about the range of motion of the arm swing.

I must confess: I am a huncher. When I began walking with the power-arm swing, I kept lifting my shoulders, tensing up. At first I thought it was my unconscious effort to keep my hands at the proper height. But from feedback I have received at many workshops, and through a bit of self-discovery, I now know that I hunch because I carry tension in my shoulders. You may carry tension there as well. If so, concentrate on keeping your shoulders down. It takes some thinking and constant adjusting, but you will have it in a week. I have found the change well worth the effort. I am more relaxed, and the power-arm swinging actually massages away tension.

Good posture, the right stride, and a power-arm swing can make for more effective and enjoyable workouts. They will also help you walk faster. Right now, you may not care about speed, but you will as you become fitter. You will need to walk faster to keep your heart rate in your target heart rate zone. You will also *want* to walk faster. It's fun to zoom. When you are really motoring, you feel absolutely free, as if you are giving your strong body a chance to do what it was built to do.

Let me offer two specific speed tips before we end the chapter. I have already mentioned that to walk faster, you increase the *number* of strides you take, not your stride *length*. You should also speed up your arm swinging. This not only gives you more forward momentum, but it also works the upper body nicely.

The other suggestion I have is to "walk the line." When you are not concerned about speed, you probably walk with your feet moving back and forth on two parallel lines. To increase your speed, try to make your feet land on one imaginary line running between your legs, repeatedly coming down one foot in front of the other. Just the inside of each foot would touch the line, if there were one; your feet should not cross over. Walking the line causes your hips to slightly turn back and forth. This action pulls powerful hip and buttock muscles into your walking stride, giving you more speed and of course building those muscles. Just a slight hip action is all you need for more speed, so don't exaggerate the motion.

Walking is a pleasant way to exercise, but you won't get a great workout if you look like a walking corpse. Get your full body into the act. I notice many mall walkers ambling around with hands in their pockets, for example, or even talking with their hands as they walk. These are the same walkers who complain that they're not losing weight, firming up the flab in their arms, or tightening their tummy muscles. What they need to do is put effort into it by getting their arms, posture, and stride length into the act.

Thought for Week 4

Next time you feel that a food craving has you cornered, fight it off with Benjamin Franklin's wise words: "It is easier to suppress the first desire than to satisfy all that follows it."

8

Week 5: Get the Walker's Mental Edge

Congratulations! You are halfway through the WalkSport Fit Forever Program. If you've been having trouble reaching your goals, you may find your excitement about mall walking and weight man–agement leveling off. You may even be thinking about quitting. Well, forget that! This week, we're going to nip that thinking in the bud.

First, I assure you that what you may be experiencing is natural. Infatuation always ends. Sadly, however, too many people end their programs when the thrill is gone. You remember Barb? She quit mall walking for a year, gained weight, and suf–fered through a winter of discontent. That was bad enough, but the suffering did not end once she returned to her program.

GOALS FOR WEEK 5:

- Mall walk five times, 25 minutes each time

- Make one walk a Power Walk

- Lose 1 pound

- Think "not perfect"

"It was hard to go back," Barb says. "I was heavier than when I stopped mall walking, and it af–fected my self-esteem. I had a difficult time walking with others I had known because I didn't want them to see me heavier."

I want to help you avoid such a setback. Comebacks are inspiring, but some people never come back and always regret having quit exercising

145

and weight management. They shake their heads at how much momentum they had going for them when they stopped, and they often wish they could have come up with a way to avoid boredom, manage time better, re-examine priorities—whatever it would have taken to help them stick with their programs.

This week I am going to help you "freshen up" your mall walking by showing you how to keep staleness away, avoid all-or-nothing thinking, and keep out of the perfectionist pit by thinking "not perfect." Your goal this week is to mall walk five times, for 25 minutes each time. Once you

MALL WALKING MAVEN

Donna's Slide

Now for a cautionary tale. Donna remembers in the fall of 1992 having a terrible time walking on a tour in Edinburgh, Scotland. "I thought I was going to die—and then I was hoping I would, because I felt so uncomfortable," she recalls. "It was awful, and I knew if I was going to continue traveling, I had to do something."

The next spring, Donna started to walk around a nearby lake. "That first month my hips hurt so badly I didn't think I would make it home," she says. But she kept going, began watching her fat intake, and the weight started falling off. The diet changes, at first, were very simple: She substituted mustard for mayonnaise on her sandwiches and later decided to give up chips. These small changes and her walking paid off: In 1 year she lost 120 pounds.

"I was looking good and feeling good. I was walking 4 miles every day, no matter what the weather. I can remember in the winter coming home with frost formed on my eyelashes—it was fantastic," she remembers.

Donna kept doing it for the next 4 years, and then she met her future husband. She started to "slide," as she puts it. She says she began being less careful about start to put in this kind of time, you sometimes need to be creative about keeping your workouts lively and fun.

Keep Staleness Away

Into every romance a little boredom shall fall. Before you let your mall walks go dull, try some of these tips to keep staleness at bay.

Do some review. Review the affirmations you created and the 29 motivational mall walking activities in chapter 3. A few of them will

what she ate, and she started missing more and more days of walking. The slide continued for 2 years. Then Donna stopped walking altogether.

"I'll admit that part of my incentive in walking was that I wanted to go out on a date," she says. "Yes, I wanted to feel good and walk during my travels, but my social life and dating were not working. So I started walking and watching what I ate, and then I got this guy who said he didn't care if I walked. We got engaged and then married. We built a house, and there was a lot of commotion and stress at the time with the house and this new family."

Donna and her husband would go on walks once in a while, but he was not as interested as she was. Also, the new suburban neighborhood had no lake or sidewalks, which reduced the enjoyment. Her husband quit smoking and started putting on weight. Donna was also putting on weight during this "slide" period, and the extra weight caused pain in her joints. By the time she quit walking, she had regained all of the 120 pounds that she lost, and then some. "When I was walking regularly, my sister and I went to Montreal and walked 10 miles around the city one day," she says. "Now I couldn't do 10 blocks."

Donna says she will return to walking—she likes the benefits of mall walking—"but it may take me 2 years to get going again," she quips.

Don't let this happen to you!

strike your fancy and get you hotfooting it. Write them in the top of your food diary this week as daily reminders.

Read to get revved. When I first started walking, my sense of commitment disappeared after 2 weeks. What got me over that hump was Casey Meyer's first book, *Aerobic Walking*. Books and magazines about fitness and weight management abound. Read them regularly for inspiration and ideas. Even if they're not about mall walking, the people featured in those books and magazines have incredible stories to tell.

Hit a different mall. Make one of your mall walking workouts this week at a different mall with a layout that appeals to you. It may have more stairs, for example, than "your" mall, and the stair workout may be the change of pace that you need once in a while. Rotate several malls into the mix as you continue mall walking. Overall, none of them may be as good as "your" mall, but you'll appreciate the variety and meet new mall walking friends.

Walk outdoors. Walking outdoors can ground you, reconnect you with your neighbors and the elements of nature, and recharge your batteries with new sights and sounds. Find a lake, park, creek, river, mountain, or hill to walk. Wear good shoes as well as clothing that will keep you warm—or, in hot weather, cool—and dry. This is not mall walking, so be careful about footing, sunscreens, allergens, critters, and all the rest that goes with walking outdoors. Also, use common sense about such personal safety concerns as walking near traffic, at night, and in high-crime areas. Be extra safe and walk with a friend.

Walking your dog is great for the both of you, and walking with the intent of feeding the birds gives you a destination and brightens your day. Or head out the door without a destination. Instead of holding a walking route in mind, make decisions on the move, based on whatever moves you at the time.

Make an excuse list. Some people, including me, are experts at making excuses and finding reasons not to walk. I would add that there is usually an answer to the excuse—a can-do response to no-can-do reasoning. Refuse to bow to the excuse and talk back to yourself, justifying how the walk *can* and *will be* done.

PENCIL TIME

Talk Back to Your Excuses

In the left column below, list your seven most common excuses for not mall walking. In the right column, "talk back" to your excuses, giving can-do statements to counter them. Next time you come up with an excuse for missing a workout, refer to the can-do column.

Excuses:	Can-do statements:
1. _____	_____
2. _____	_____
3. _____	_____
4. _____	_____
5. _____	_____
6. _____	_____
7. _____	_____

Go "inside." Instead of rushing to fill each moment of your workout with sizzle, let things simmer down. The rhythmic, repetitive nature of walking is perfect for going "inside," centering yourself and focusing your thinking on creative ideas or solutions to problems. Your creativity and problem-solving can range from "What do I really want out of life?" to "How can I find the time this week to paint the garage?"

Hit the laugh track. Laughing is fun, free, and makes you feel good. It is also good for you and your heart. Studies show that frequent laughter—the harder the better—may lower blood pressure, increase protective antibodies, help the immune system, reduce stress, and lower heart disease risk. Researchers believe laughter helps minimize inflammation in the blood vessels, which decreases the risk of blood clots.

A study from the University of Maryland Medical Center tested the "humor quotient" of 300 people and found that those with heart disease were 40 percent less likely to recognize humor or use it to get out of uncomfortable situations than their healthy counterparts. They generally laughed less and displayed more anger and hostility than most people.

Make laughter part of your mall walking workout. As you walk, think of funny things you did or saw that day. You may have raced out the door this morning wearing different-colored socks, or you buttoned your shirt "one button off" and didn't know it until someone told you at work. Chuckle about it. Recall a comical scene in a movie or a funny line in a book. Listen to a Garrison Keillor or Bill Cosby audiotape while you walk. Come to the mall with a joke, and share it with others. Or try laughing by design. Laugh in threes (ha-ha-ha, ha-ha-ha, ha-ha-ha) continuously for 1 minute. It's called fake it till you make it. Hearing your own laughter can induce real laughter. You may look kind of funny in the mall, but then you and your friends will *really* have something to laugh about.

Change your Power Walks. So far your Power Walks have consisted of mall walking mixed with squats, pushups, rows, wall crunches, and bent-over leg extensions. This week, and in the weeks to come, rotate new exercises into the mix. Try the six extra exercises in "More WalkSport Fit Forever Power Walk Exercises," on page 152.

Avoid All-or-Nothing Thinking

More often than not, all-or-nothing thinking derails people from their exercise and weight management programs. They are on track as long as they put forth their all and do all that the program offers. But when—not if—they have a slip, the illusion of their perfectionism is busted and they do nothing. "What's the use?" they lament.

Donna was doing all she could, walking 4 miles every day and dropping weight weekly. "I was driven," she says of her heyday of walking and weight management. "I was obsessed with healthy food, and I panicked if I couldn't get in my daily walk." As long as she was in her "all" mode, she was fine. But when marriage, a sudden family, and a new house derailed her from doing it all, she rode the slippery slide to "nothing"—and regained the 120 pounds she had lost.

"It used to be when my husband and I disagreed, we'd go for a walk and talk about it," Donna says. "But when we stopped walking, instead he would go to the garage and smoke, and I would go to the kitchen and eat."

Donna's most important lesson was to stop thinking in absolute terms. "The way I had been doing it, I had no wiggle room. If I made an error, I thought I could not recover from it. I was so obsessed, I believed I couldn't miss one workout or eat any fatty foods. Now, I know if you have a slip, you get back up and keep going. You don't beat yourself up."

Think about that word "slip." Slipping in an exercise-and-weight-management program is like slipping on ice. You don't mean to slip. You don't slip because you are bad or weak. You may slip because you get a little careless, inattentive, or overwhelmed, perhaps, but mostly you slip because ice is slippery. It is simply hard not to fall sometimes, just as it is hard not to fall with exercise and weight management.

After you fall on ice, you probably laugh about being human, and then get back up. You don't berate yourself, because you know lots of people fall on ice. The same should be true with my program. When you have a slip and fall, I would love it if you chuckle about being human and then get back up and go at your program again. Your slip of chowing down samples of every chocolate dessert at your choir's potluck dinner cost you, what, an extra 1,000 or 2,000 calories? In the course of an 8-week program such as this, those calories are insignificant. What *is* significant is your attitude about those calories. With an all-or-nothing attitude, your reaction is ruinous. With a wiggle-room attitude, your reaction is to be easy on yourself but keep going forward—the healthiest, longest-lasting, most human reaction. Perfect doesn't exist, in *anything*.

Think "Not Perfect"

All-or-nothing thinking is perfectionism that is polluting your head. I want to help you clean up that pollution and get the most out of my program. Here are several suggestions to help you think "not perfect."

(continued on page 154)

More WalkSport Fit Forever Power Walk Exercises

Stair Climb

A great way to build up your glutes and thighs is simply to walk the stairs at the mall. (You may also be able to use the escalators; often they are not moving early in the morning.) Several studies show that people who took stairs instead of elevators or escalators improved their overall fitness by 10 to 15 percent. And one study found that people who climbed 50 stairs or more each day had a reduced risk of heart disease.

Lunge

This exercise builds glutes and thighs and also is good for developing balance and posture. Place your right foot 2 to 3 feet in front of you. Bend your right knee. As you do so, drop your left knee toward the floor. Your left heel will come off the floor. Make sure your right knee is directly over your right ankle. Don't lean forward. Hold, and then push yourself back up. Repeat with your left leg in front.

Note: If you have knee problems, skip lunges and do squats instead, making sure your knees are bent less than 90 degrees.

Wall Pushup with Leg Extension

This exercise works the arms and chest, and also the lower back muscles. Place your palms, shoulder-width apart, on a wall. Step back into a comfortable standing pushup position. Make sure your feet won't slip and you are not leaning at an angle so steep that you will not be able to perform a wall pushup. Slowly bend your elbows and move your chest toward the wall. As you hold this position, extend your right leg backward, lifting with the heel. Lower your right leg, and repeat with the left leg. With both feet back on the floor, straighten your arms to complete the wall pushup.

Heel Raise

Heel raises are simple and effective in building calf muscles. Stand with your feet hip-width apart. Using a bench or wall for support and balance, rise onto your toes. Hold, and then slowly lower. As you become stronger, try doing heel raises one leg at a time.

Bent-Leg V Sit

This exercise works your abdominal muscles, hips, thighs, shoulders, and back of the arms. Sit on a bench or the floor. Lean back slightly, supporting your body with both hands. Your fingers should be spread, thumbs forward, and your elbows slightly bent. Bend your knees and pull both toward your chest, contracting stomach muscles and keeping toes at the same level as your knees. To work the abs more from this position, point your toes and lower one foot toward the ground, keeping the knee bent. Bring the knee back to the chest. Repeat with the opposite leg.

Bench Dip with Knee Extension

This type of dip works the muscles of the chest, back of the upper arms, and thighs. Sit on the edge of a bench or sturdy chair. Make sure the bench or chair will not budge during the exercise. Firmly grip the edge, and slowly lift your buttocks off the bench. Your legs should be together and knees bent. Extend your left leg straight out at the knee. Repeat with the right leg.

As you become stronger, try this version of the exercise: After you slowly lift your buttocks off the bench, lower yourself slowly toward the floor. Your elbows will bend backward as you dip. Start by dipping only an inch or so before straightening your arms again. Gradually dip deeper and deeper as you become stronger. Finish the dip with knee extensions, one leg at a time.

Set realistic yet challenging goals. If you set your goals too high—losing 100 pounds in 6 months, for example—you are not allowing any room for error. As Donna says, you need wiggle room. If you set your goals too low, like mall walking just twice a week, it will be easy to be perfect week after week. But this perfectionism holds you back because you will not come to understand that failure is ultimately a way of expanding and teaching you. Failure is a necessary prerequisite to success.

Stop comparing. Comparison is the quickest route to shame, and shame is what drives perfectionists. You don't get extra credit for walking faster than everyone else in your mall walking club or demerits if you walk slower. This program is as personal as your health, so stop the comparisons. Strive for excellence, not superiority; progress, not perfection.

Never say never. Okay, I broke the rule already. That proves I am not perfect, right? My point is that these imperative words—never, always, must, every, each—allow for no wiggle room. These words bring to mind the inner drill sergeant who demands perfection—or else. Tell your inner sergeant to chill, then work at weeding out imperative words in your conversations. For example, instead of saying "I will never miss a day of mall walking," change to, "I will reach my goal of mall walking daily. If I don't because of an emergency, I won't beat myself up about it."

Think of perfectionism as your oppressor. We often glorify perfectionism, thinking it will bring out the best in us. I believe just the opposite. Perfectionism is a burden, a deceitful oppressor that limits us and keeps fun at the fringes of life. Perfectionists obsess about external rewards, the only things that seem to satisfy them. They are often people pleasers, rigid, intolerant of failure (especially in themselves), and procrastinators. They tend to dwell on negative outcomes, have their self-worth chained to their achievements, and carry a play-it-safe attitude. They can be indecisive, pessimistic, and constantly frustrated. Frankly, they're not much fun.

Don't place all your eggs in one basket. Focus on your primary goal, but don't lose sight of the rewards of the journey *toward* your goal. You may never lose those 30 pounds, for example, but your quest has some pretty cool by-products. You may look and feel better, your blood pressure may be down, and your social life may be up. Learning to appreciate these by-products reduces the stress, anxiety, and tension that are caused by your quest. As a result, on your way to reaching your primary goal, you travel lighter, experiencing more joy and fulfillment along the way.

A Slip Is Not a Slide

In this chapter, I have been trying to help you cut some slack for yourself. I want you to understand that my program has room for some wiggle. You are allowed some slips—as long as the slips don't string together to become a Donna-like slide.

As we reach the end of Week 5, I want you to plan for your slips. They will happen, so you might as well prepare for them. Without a plan, you may be tempted to throw up your hands when you slip and say something like, "Here we go again," or "What's the use—I've blown it now."

PENCIL ✎ TIME

What Can You Do Besides Eat?

List eight activities you can do when you are tempted to overeat. Go to this list when you have slipped and sense that a slide is coming on.

1. _____
2. _____
3. _____
4. _____
5. _____
6. _____
7. _____
8. _____

Write your Slip Plan in your diary, and earmark that page for quick reference. You can make up your own plan or use this one.

Be suspicious. Ask yourself if the slip was just a slip or a warning sign of an impending slide. Are there social situations or friends that you need to avoid, rooms in your home where you always pig out, or feelings that lead to overeating? Get feedback from others as well, and write a strategy for those times your intuition shouts, "Danger!"

Be cool. The "Here we go again" kinds of statements come when you lose your cool, heap blame on yourself, and make matters worse than they are.

Find a slips friend. Prepare her in advance that you will be calling and would like encouragement, not blame. Your slips friend can remind you of how far you've come and of your original resolve to mall walk and manage your weight. Take each occurrence as a new chance to make a better choice.

Take immediate action. Don't overanalyze. You have a pretty good idea what the problems are, so address them ASAP. For example, you may be eating too much pepperoni and sausage pizza, so get rid of your pizza coupons and refrigerator magnets that allow you to easily call for delivery.

List alternative activities. Doing these activities instead of eating will pull you out of a potential slide because they are bold signals that you are not going to just lie down and slide. Such activities could include going to a museum, reading a thriller, and going to a movie. Take a moment to create your own list of alternative activities.

Thought for Week 5

If you find yourself trying to be perfect with the WalkSport Fit Forever Program, think of Mae West. She would have been my kind of mall walker, based on this line: "I used to be Snow White . . . but I drifted."

9

Week 6: Building Healthy Habits

"Habits are at first cobwebs, then cables." This Spanish proverb is the best depiction of developing new habits that I've ever heard. I hope you have swept out the unhealthy cobwebs and replaced them with healthy cables.

By the beginning of Week 6, you are in the habit of mall walking, doing 30-minute walks five times this week. Make one of those a Power Walk, walking five 5-minute walking intervals separated by the 1 minute special strength exercises described in Weeks 3 and 5.

Warming up, stretching, cooling down, good walking form, and working out in your target training zones should be habitual to you at this point. Planning your food for the week and recording what you eat in your diary should be second nature as well.

Sometimes habits can be a little bit more challenging to develop. This week, we'll talk about how to make them "stick." Among the most powerful of these are finding a program partner, slowing your eating rate, and finding ways to stop stress eating.

GOALS FOR WEEK 6:

- Mall walk five times, 30 minutes each time

- Make one walk a Power Walk

- Lose 1 pound

- Slow your eating rate

Make Healthy Habits

Would you untie your shoes for me? Thanks. Now tie them. Easy, right? You could do this with your eyes closed, underwater, upside-down, or in a raging gale. You are good at it, you can do it quickly and efficiently, and you don't have to think about it as you do it. You just do it.

Now, try explaining how to tie a shoe to a child. You'd better set aside at least 15 minutes, several times, because learning a new habit such as this isn't easy (especially that last part about making a "tree" with the lace so the "bunny" goes around the tree then through the tree, before you pull the two bunny ears tight). The child may be able to learn to tie from you, but he will need time and practice before becoming proficient. In the meantime, he'll be painfully slow at tying shoes, as any parent who has stood at the door tapping a toe while a little one insists on tying his own shoes knows. But in time, the parent doesn't have to wait, because the child has made a habit out of tying and can do it lickety-split.

Habits are a big help when they are good for you. But if you smoke, "forget" to mall walk, or eat a dozen Oreos each night, you're obviously into some habits that you should abandon. Habits are hard to make, but they're even harder to break.

Changing your bad habits to good ones frees you up from scores of small decisions, leaving your mind less cluttered for the more important choices. For example, first thing in the morning, I put on my walking clothes, preparing to go to the mall. I don't even think about it. I just walk on autopilot to the closet and do it. During these 8 weeks, I am trying to help you develop new habits concerning mall walking and weight management. Once these things become habits, you no longer have to expend precious brain power thinking about them—they'll be as familiar as breathing. Try these extra ways to firm up the good changes you're making now.

Study your elders. A great way to increase your awareness of the power of habits is to study older adults. Shari has been motivated to mall walk by the example of her 90-year-old grandmother, who has exercised for her entire life. She also gets inspired when she sees the dedication of older mall walkers who work out with the aid of their walkers.

Try this: Observe one group of older adults that makes a habit out of exercise and weight management and then a second group that doesn't. Which group do you want to belong to later in life? "I figure you have to take time to exercise and stay fit now, or you better plan on time to be sick as you get older," Shari says.

Ask: "When do I feel good?" Most mall walkers feel out of sorts when they don't do their daily workout. "I really don't feel good unless I exercise," mall walker Geri says. "I feel stronger, as if I have been given a gift that day. Mall walking has just become a part of my life."

You may have noticed that out-of-sorts feeling on days you have not walked. Trust that feeling, and use the memory of it to help you develop good eating and exercise habits.

Hang with good-habits people. "Winning is a habit," Vince Lombardi, the legendary Green Bay Packers coach, said. "Unfortunately, so is losing." When you pal around with winners—people with habits that lead to success—the winner inside you comes out. But you make it really tough on yourself to lose weight if you spend time with people who pound down several six-packs of beer each week. To establish good mall walking and weight management habits, make sure your friends have the habits you aspire to.

Friends are especially important to men who want to make exercise a habit, according to an Ohio State study of more than 900 college-age people. Women, on the other hand, were more likely to be regular exercisers if their families encouraged them to be active.

Practice, and practice patience. You've had a lifetime for your old habits to take root. To uproot them, you may need more than the 8 weeks in this program. A 30-year-old person has eaten nearly 33,000 meals. That's a lot of practice, so you'll need a lot more practice to change your eating habits. You won't need 33,000 meals, but you will need to be patient. When developing good habits, take the advice of Ralph Waldo Emerson: "Adopt the pace of nature: Her secret is patience."

Find a Program Partner

Sometimes habits can form around the people you walk with, not just the exercise. A program partner is someone with whom you can mall walk and set weight management goals. Partners lift each other up, providing a pleasant distraction during walks, and motivate each other to stick with the program.

I'm all for program partnerships, but keep in mind that partnerships are not for everyone. Some prefer the solitude of walking solo. I choose both ways. Sometimes I like to go solo, to reflect and sort out personal matters in my head. But other times I like to be pushed by a partner, and challenge her in turn. I also like the encouragement and support I receive from a partner when I'm just not doing as well as I would hope. But I'm a competitive person, and I must admit, I can sometimes get sucked into petty, unspoken contests with partners that can become annoying and counterproductive.

Try it both ways to see if you want a program partner or not. Maybe you will want both options, so seek out a partner with a like mind. Maybe you will want to partner with your spouse. You definitely want someone who is as motivated as you are; you don't want to be "carrying" your partner. You also want someone who is like you. If you like to compete, find a competitive partner. If you have an "in-your-face" style, find a partner who will be in your face when you start slacking off. If you have a softer style, make sure your partner has the same style. Think about the type of partner with whom you will be comfortable. Consider collecting a pool of partners. For example, you could have a competitive one for the times you want to compete, a confidante partner for sharing your inner struggles, and a motivating partner on whom you can rely to perk you up.

Now that you have a program partner (or partners), work with that person. I recommend going for a mall walk then talking over lunch. Bring your diary and define your collaboration. Be open and honest, asking for exactly what you want out of the partnership. These three questions can help you clarify the biggest issues.

PENCIL TIME

List Some Possible Program Partners

If you want to try a program partnership, list five potential partners in the left column below. In the middle column, note why each person would be a good match for you. Discuss the potential partnership with the people on your list. In the third column, record their responses.

Name	Why this person?	Response

How much of a commitment is necessary? The partnership can be as simple as meetings for mall walking and discussions about weight management. You may agree to call each other between walks, become goal buddies, share recipes, and go to movies. One partner may agree to be a role model for the other. You may decide to go grocery shopping together so that you can help each other resist the no-no foods you know you shouldn't buy. Be very clear about your expectations of commitment from each other.

Are each of us comfortable making specific requests? This should not be a mind reading relationship. A partnership can be a powerful tool in this program, especially when it addresses your specific needs. Can you ask for praise from your partner? Is it okay to get on each other a bit when you have done poorly with your programs? Are you fine with asking your partner not to order that French silk pie when you have lunch together?

Think about what you will need from this partnership, and then ask for it respectfully and positively.

How will we reward each other? Each of you may have different ideas on when a reward is appropriate. For example, you may be surprised when your beaming partner thrusts a wrapped gift in your hand at the end of your first week in the program, your reward for completing Week 1. You may like the idea of rewards but believe they should come after doing something more significant than completing 1 week. Rewards are important and fun, so brainstorm ideas of when and how you will reward each other. That way you'll be prepared and avoid one of you always being the beaming-but-wondering giver while the other is the embarrassed-and-feeling-like-a-bonehead receiver.

Slow Your Eating

Geri, my mall walking friend you met earlier in the chapter, is one of those people you admire but . . . well, "hate" is too strong a word, because Geri is so nice. But she has never had a weight problem. She has good genes going for her. She watches what she eats, consuming lots of fruits and vegetables, and she's always on the lookout for fatty foods. And she mall walks almost daily for about an hour.

Geri has a lot going for her, but one other thing about Geri that has helped her manage her weight is that she eats slowly. "Whenever I go out to eat with others, I am generally the last at the table to finish my meal," she says. "My family is the same way—we like good food, but that is not our focus. Some people live to eat, but I eat to live."

I like that distinction. We tend to live our lives on fast-forward. Hitting "pause" to eat slowly sounds divinely relaxing. Nutritionists say eating slowly is also sound advice for weight management. Eating fast reduces your enjoyment of food, but it also overwhelms your internal fullness mechanism, with the end result being overeating.

As you eat, your body sends signals to your brain when the stomach becomes full. Experts say it takes about 20 minutes for the brain to "get it," to figure out that you are done eating. Eating quickly means you can pack in a lot of food—often too much—before your 20 minutes are up. By the time you're satiated and you put down your fork, the overeating damage is done; you are painfully full of food and extra calories.

Several factors contribute to satiety, according to Kay Guidarelli, R.D., L.D., a consultant and dietitian in Minneapolis. Two obvious factors are taste and volume of food. Another is the number of foods eaten in a meal. If you just eat pizza, Guidarelli says, you don't feel as full as when you eat pizza with salad, milk, and dessert. Texture can be a factor; sometimes you don't feel full until you have eaten something crunchy or smooth. You may also not feel sated if the temperature of your food is wrong. For example, a cold sandwich in winter may not fill you up, but hot soup will. Another factor is what is already in your gastrointestinal system. Say you filled up on pizza Friday night. A friend invites you to lunch on Saturday, and she serves lasagna. Because you had pizza, a similar food, the night before, you will feel fuller faster on lasagna than if she served fish.

Guidarelli says the type of food you eat determines how quickly you feel full and how long the fullness lasts. She explains that the satisfaction from eating high-sugar foods lasts only 30 to 60 minutes, and then you feel hungry again. A mix of starches and sugars satisfies you for 2 to 2½ hours. Add protein and the satisfaction can last 3 to 4 hours. Finally, if you add fat to a sugar, starch, and protein meal, the satisfaction lasts 4 to 5 hours or longer.

This principle does suggest why avoiding fat to reduce calorie intake *can* backfire. For example, Guidarelli says eating no-fat cookies gives you a healthy snack, but you will be hungry again in 30 minutes or so. You may be tempted to eat more cookies, which, by the way, still contain calories. So you may have trimmed your fat intake, but your calorie count is rising. Swinging to the other extreme, people who eat a high-protein and high-fat meal may think they will be satisfied for up to 5 hours and will therefore eat fewer calories. The problem, says Guidarelli, is that protein and fat don't satisfy you as quickly as sugar and starch. So, while you are waiting for satisfaction, you may overeat. She says the best strategy for sustained satisfaction is to eat a mixed meal so that the sugars kick in early, followed by a series of satisfying waves of starches, proteins, and then fats.

"One of my clients, a teacher, said she dieted during the day and she still couldn't lose weight," says Guidarelli. "I asked her what her evening food plan was, and she said she didn't have one; she just ate all night because she was never full. It took her 2½ years to break that pattern, but I helped her to structure her evening meals so they included sugar, starch, proteins, and fats. This type of meal satisfied her, so she stopped grazing. I also advised her to eat an afternoon snack, distribute calories more evenly throughout the day, and walk four to five times a week. She lost 30 pounds in 7 months."

I come from a large family, and I have to admit that there were times when I ate fast because I worried that there would be little left for me if I didn't—especially seconds on the good stuff. Your challenge is to break this habit and slow down. Try these seven tips to help you slow down your eating and enjoy your meal more.

Wash your hands before eating. This makes eating a ritual, and it is also sanitary.

Give thanks. Offering a prayer of thanks for your food elevates the meal and reminds you to appreciate and savor it.

Schedule meals and snacks. If you spread eating times evenly throughout the day, you arrive at meals hungry, but not ravenous. With an eating schedule, you are less likely to wolf down food and more likely to eat slowly.

Put your hands together. After you put a bite of food into your mouth, put down your fork, put your hands together on your lap, and chew the food completely. Swallow, then pick up the fork for another bite. If you are eating a sandwich or other finger food, put the food down between bites and put your hands together.

Take a midmeal break. Partway through your meal, stop eating for 30 seconds. After a few days, increase your break times to maybe 3 minutes. Fill the time with reflection or conversation. If the food gets cold, heat it again. An interesting study done on animals found that interrupting meals meant that fewer calories were eaten, even though the animals could eat freely after the break.

Just eat. Distractions like watching TV or reading while you eat can lead to overeating. You just keep shoving food into your mouth during the TV program's chase scene. Instead, concentrate on eating, and taste every bite. Feel the different textures. Smell the food's aroma. Separating eating from other activities diminishes the power of these activities to stimulate eating.

Pick one spot to eat. Don't graze all over your home, literally eating on the run. I admit I don't do this one very well. Sometimes I eat two meals a day in my car and just one at my table. Pick one spot and make it the sole place to eat. Settle in, slow down, and enjoy.

Eat Less during Stress

When I think about stress I think of Donna, whom you met last week. She walked every day, lost 120 pounds, and then stress hit: She got married, built a house, and suddenly became a stepparent to her husband's four children. All good things, but still major stresses. She was thrown off her program and regained all the weight she had lost.

Some people lose weight because of stress, but many others, like Donna, put it on. They do this for many reasons. Some become distracted and don't pay attention to what, or how much, they eat. Others feel that their lives are so tough, they deserve to self-soothe with food. Still others feel a deadline pressure and overeat because they think they need extra energy or it helps them focus. All these very compelling habits are very hard to break, but perhaps the best strategy is to tackle them at the source.

Reduce your stress. You are probably saying, "Well, duh!" Everyone knows that when you have too much stress you should do your best to reduce it. That's true, but too many of us accept high levels of stress because we think that everyone has stress and we can handle it. Often, we only realize we cannot handle stress when we wake up one morning and realize we are 100 pounds heavier than we were last year.

Don't underestimate or ignore stress. It can get you. Stress management programs, books, and tapes burst with relaxation skills and stress reduction techniques. Check them out, and consider them weight loss strategies on their own.

Fight stress with other distractions. Remember your list of alternative activities to eating? Go to this list when you have just finished a nasty conversation with your boss, are preparing for a tax audit, or are engaged in other such stressful situations and are tempted by food. The most obvious positive alternative I can think of is mall walking. Often when I get stressed out, I grab my shoes and head to the mall.

Try a short period of relaxation first. Rather than using food to numb your stress, spend a few minutes in meditation or just relaxing. Go into your breathing room, or just take a few deep breaths. It will help you calm down. Also, you'll see that you *can* handle stress in ways other than eating.

Record the number of times you say "yes." In your diary, make a list of the times you say "yes" to requests from other people this week, no matter how minor. Write a word or two about the situation and then answer this question: "Did I really *want* to say 'yes?'" My guess is your stress is less during the weeks that you said "yes" only when you really wanted to. So, say "yes" when you really mean it and practice saying "no"—to food you don't want and people you're not especially inspired to spend time with. Carving out this time for you alone will create a cushion you can relax within, a stress-free zone that protects your best intentions!

Thought for Week 6

In this chapter, we learned that being patient with yourself is key in forming new habits, slowing your pace of eating, and reducing stress. So I will leave you with Lily Tomlin's words: "For fast-acting relief, try slowing down."

10

Week 7: Sass Your Inner Ogre

$\int$ometimes I'm my own worst enemy."

Have you ever said that? I certainly have. I'll rip into myself for only walking for 30 minutes if I wanted to do 45. Of course, nothing was wrong with 30 minutes—it's just not 45. That's just one small example of how I can focus on what I *didn't* do versus what I *did* do. If these sorts of small rips start bunching together into a major tear, I develop this absolutely lousy feeling that I can only explain as, "I'm never quite where I want to be."

In this chapter, I'll offer a pep talk for people who, like me, tend to be overly self-critical. This tendency can backfire on your weight loss goals, especially when you let it influence your body image. We'll talk about how to preserve a strong body image, and also, how family support can help you get through rough times. In order to keep up your healthy eating momentum, I'll share some of my favorite food shopping, storing, and serving strategies. But first, let's take a moment to further refine your program to *you*.

GOALS FOR WEEK 7:

• Mall walk six times, 30 minutes each time

• Make two of your walks Power Walks: alternate 5 minutes of walking and 1 minute of exercising five times, for a total of 30 minutes

• Recruit family support

• Lose 1 pound

Time to Tweak

You are now, at Week 7, in the "tweaking" stage of the program. That is, you have your basic program down, but you are making adjustments here and there to meet your needs. For example, what if you want to get in a workout but your time is limited? Have you started hitting the stairs or escalators (come before business hours, when escalators are not running) at the mall, the office, or home? Stair work quickly gets your heart rate up into your training zone.

Do you find that you want to do more speed workouts because you know they can help you burn more calories and lose weight? If so, first check to make sure you are maintaining good form. You tend to make two common mistakes when you try to go faster: leaning forward and swinging your power arms too far across your body. Second, check your pulse frequently, or wear a heart rate monitor to make sure you stay safely within your training zone. Third, make up speed games. Go fast past the food court, slow between Sears and Nordstrom, then fast again for the rest of the lap, for example. Make a tape of alternating fast and slow songs, and walk to the beat of each song. Or walk behind two or more of your friends and then turn on the speed to pass them. Keep this going, so the last walker in line keeps turning on the burners to pass the people in front.

Do you want to do more strength training? One way to do this is to increase the number of repetitions you do in 1 minute with each of the Power Walk exercises. I also recommend signing up for a strength training class at a YMCA, YWCA, or health club. You will learn to do safe workouts with spotters there to watch your technique and form.

A Pep Talk

Every program has its share of ups and downs, and it's easy to become self-critical during the downs. But harsh self-criticism sets you up for failure, because you begin searching for ways to confirm whatever comes out of your mouth. You may begin to abandon and distrust yourself. Sure, you may say, you don't really mean it when you blurt out, "I can never get anything right!" or "I'm in terrible shape," or "I'm not good enough." Well, then why do you say it?

To those of you who are self-critical, I want you to stop, already. Enough. Ripping yourself because you have not lost enough weight or are not meeting fitness goals is counterproductive. Here are six ways to sass back to your self-critical inner ogre.

Be a caddie. Have you ever eavesdropped on conversations between a golfer and his caddie? Good caddies are always encouraging, calm, and supportive. They are willing to do whatever they can to help their golfer perform at his best. Caddies don't sugarcoat matters when things are not going well—they don't say "good shot" when it was not, but they certainly don't rip, either. They try to keep their golfer in the present, reminding him of strengths and focusing on the only shot the golfer can do anything about—the next one. So, the next time you start getting self-critical, split yourself in two and pretend you are your own caddie.

Reconsider rewards. I am all for rewards and have already explained their importance. One problem with rewards, however, is that some people come to depend on them too much. They won't do something unless they give themselves, or are given, a tangible reward for outcomes. The focus then rests more on the external, on the here-today-gone-to-morrow reward, and less on the inner joy of just doing the activity. This is a setup for frustration and self-criticism because external rewards are fleeting even when you get them. To stop your self-criticism, downplay external rewards and shift your focus to affirmations and feeling good about the *internal* progress you're making.

Be your own best friend. Before criticizing yourself, ask "Would I say that to my best friend?" I doubt that you would call a friend a loser, so don't call yourself one either. Discipline your thoughts and words.

Be less critical of others. Next time you think about something your husband or friend did wrong, balance it mentally with one thing you respect about him or her. If you get into the habit of giving others a break, you will be more likely to give yourself a break as well.

Say "thanks." When self-critical people receive a compliment, many respond by saying, "Oh, it was nothing," or "I was just lucky." Instead of minimizing your achievements or brushing aside compliments, take in the kind words, swallow, and say, "Thanks, I appreciate that." With practice, it will become easier!

Record your remarks. In your diary, write down every self-critical word you say for 1 week. That's right, every time you zing yourself, pull out the diary and write it down. After a day or two of this, you'll get so sick of writing—and seeing the ugly things you say to yourself on paper—that you will surely watch your mouth the rest of the week.

Body Image Basics

Some people start exercise and weight management programs because they say they want "a new body." They may believe that thin, attractive people have perfect lives, that their appearance is responsible for the bad things that happen to them, and that if only they looked like this celebrity or that sports star they would be happy and successful.

Health—not perfect looks—should be your primary reason for doing my program. I like Shari's attitude. She walks for her health and weight management, yet at 5 feet 4 inches and 154 pounds Shari feels that she is 35 pounds heavier than she should be. "But I don't hate my body," Shari says. "I still put on a swimsuit and go to the beach with the kids."

Shari keeps working to manage her weight, but she clearly is not obsessed with getting "a new body." If you are, then you may want to consider ways of changing your body image rather than changing your body.

Take a reality test. Are your assumptions about the happiness and success of those "beautiful people" really true? Do all thin, attractive people have perfect lives? Do you know heavy people who are happy and prosperous? When that bad thing happened to you, such as losing out on a promotion, were factors involved other than your appearance? Conversely, when good things have happened to you, such as a promotion you earned, were they the result of your looks or some inner quality?

Do a realistic assessment of yourself. Ask a trusted friend to help, because sometimes you may look in the mirror and exaggerate what you don't like, or see one negative feature and think your entire self is also unattractive. Look at every physical feature of your body—feet, fingers, nose, eyes, everything—and ask yourself if you find it attractive. If you were to make a scorecard of the attractive versus unattractive features, I am sure your attractive features would win.

Once you finish assessing your physical self, do the same for your nonphysical attributes—your sense of humor, kindness, integrity, and other features that are a central part of the real you. Again, I am confident that your attractive features outnumber the unattractive ones.

Do yoga and mall walking. Yoga is great for accepting your body image, because it is a meditative exercise that causes you to center yourself and be in your body. Therapists say some people with body image problems have disassociated from their bodies because they may have been cruelly teased or sexually violated. Yoga, and especially its rhythmic breathing, helps people reconnect with their bodies and learn to like them again. (I would add that the same may be true of mall walking, which also features rhythmic breathing and a meditative state.)

Trace your body outline. Spread a large piece of paper on the floor and have a friend trace a line all around your body. Seeing that outline gives you feedback about your proportions. You may think your waist is too big, but once you see it on paper, you may realize that it's fine. Experts say seeing your outline on paper is different from looking in a mirror, which tends to confound the impression you're receiving with clothing and hairstyles—as well as "mirror, mirror on the wall" vanity!

Be current. Body image problems can develop if you try to hold onto your teenage body for too long. Instead, look around at other 30 somethings, 50-somethings, or whatever-something you are and work on accepting the norm in your age group.

Get help. Body image can become a very complex issue, so you may want to consult with a psychotherapist who specializes in working with body image and eating disorders. Also, books like *Transforming Body Image: Love the Body You Have* by Marcia Germaine Hutchinson, Ed.D., and *The Body Image Workbook* by Thomas F. Cash, Ph.D., are excellent resources.

The Importance of Family Support

In many families, if you are trying to lose weight, you are mocked or resented by the rest of the family. Silence may be as good a form of support as you are going to get. Or your relatives may become uncomfortable about what foods *they* eat when you dine with them.

Even worse, some family members may openly sabotage any efforts you are making to improve your health. They may be jealous of your success and pressure you to "let your guard down, just this once, and live a little." They may bring up past failures or serve foods they know have previously been your downfall. As you lose weight and take on an appearance that is different from the rest of the family, these saboteurs may even say that you are being disloyal to the family or that you look sick.

My advice in these family food feuds is to be firm in your resolve, but polite. Before family gatherings, practice refusal lines like, "I'd love some pie, but I ate too much corn on the cob." You may have to avoid family members or gatherings for a while, until you feel comfortable asserting yourself. Try to understand that your family's lack of support is less about ginia in her three-bedroom rambler: cut her lawn, clean windows, paint walls, weed gardens, and fill bird feeders. They moved her washer and dryer up from the basement so she could do her laundry with less hassle. They even pay for her newspaper, Internet service, and cell phone.

This kind of family support frees Virginia to go to the mall to walk. "I take my grandkids with me," she says. "They know that when they are with Grandma at the mall, they walk."

Two of her children have also started walking, and the whole family is following in Virginia's footsteps with watching what they eat. "I'll often get cards that say, 'Thanks for being a great role model,'" she says.

When someone in the family has a lapse with their weight management, "we tell each other about it," says Virginia. "We do it in a nice way, though."

What a wonderful example of how good health can be a family affair. As the matriarch, Virginia sets the pace in her family. In response, the family has not only encouraged and supported her as she maintains good health, but they have given her the highest compliment: They have followed her example.

your change and more about their fear of change. Give them time—they may decide to join you in your efforts to exercise and manage your weight.

Instead of thinking of them as the enemy, try recruiting support from family members. They know where you've been and can help you get where you want to go as well as, or better, than anyone. If you ask for your family's help, they may surprise you—and themselves.

Food Shopping, Storing, and Serving Strategies

The entire trip from the grocery store to the table is a minefield of challenges. Highly paid people at food manufacturers and grocery stores plot behind closed doors to get you to buy their high-priced, high-fat foods.

Even if you only cave in to temptation a bit, and buy mostly healthy foods, how you store food in your home makes a huge difference in what you end up eating. Then, once you sit down to eat, more challenges arise.

Shopping Strategies

Many people think their problems with weight management begin when they sit down at the table to eat. I would argue that they begin when you set foot in a grocery store. After all, what you buy is what you eat.

When you have problem foods under your roof, you are more apt to eat them when you have a slip—and then pay for it later. But if you have a lot of salad fixings and fruits on hand, your slip won't be such a big deal, because you can hardly get into trouble by eating too many carrots and mangos. As in most good habits, planning is the best strategy.

Shop on a full stomach. When you are hungry, everything looks good, especially high-fat fare. If you're not hungry, it's easier to make healthier purchases. Also, shopping from a list helps cut down on impulse purchases. It's easiest to make your shopping list right after you've made your weekly meal plan in your diary—which is best not to do when you're hungry, either! (One more suggestion: Take a set amount of cash with you to the grocery store. When you pay with cash, you are more careful about not straying from your shopping list.)

Allow plenty of time to shop. You make better decisions when you aren't rushed. When you're in a hurry, you might be tempted to buy instant foods, such as microwaveable meals and prepackaged foods. Because they're so packed with extra fillers, these foods are notoriously unsatisfying. You may be tempted to scarf down one meal, impulsively prepare a second, and suck that one down as well. When you have to prepare a meal from scratch, you're less likely to finish it and head back to the stove to repeat the cutting and cooking for a second round of grub.

Choose with care. Really think before putting food in your cart. Shop the outer walls of the grocery store, and fill your cart with fruits and vegetables first. Avoid packaged foods that have added sugar. Soups are filling, satisfying, inexpensive, convenient, and easy to make. They also work as a snack, as part of a meal, or as a cooking ingredient. Pick interesting sauces, condiments, and marinades, which are great for adding flavor, moisture, texture, and versatility to your meals. Light dressings and dips can also perk up plain veggies. And don't forget to treat yourself to lower calorie desserts, such as sorbets or individually packaged frozen bars.

Storing Strategies

Your ability to regulate when and how much you eat is also dictated by *where* you store food in your home. Stashing your food so that it's more convenient to make healthy choices is the key.

Put tempting snacks away. If food is in sight, it will soon be in mouth. When bowls of salted nuts, candy, or chips are near your favorite TV chair, I challenge you to sit and *not* mindlessly eat. The temptation is too great. I must admit that I have a bowl of M&Ms by my entryway (Welcome to Sara's fitness sanctuary!), but at least they are not near my TV chair. If these treats are stored behind the pantry door or someplace else out of sight, you're less likely to want to get a handful of nuts once you are in your comfort zone after a long day at the office. Even if you momentarily weaken and succumb to the urge, you still have time to come to your senses during your walk from the TV room to the pantry.

Better yet, hide them. Put that half-gallon of toffee coffee ice cream in the back of the freezer, behind the frozen peas and spinach, where you won't see it each time you open the door. Similarly, hide chips and cookies high and back in the cupboard behind the seldom-used Crock-Pot. Store tempting treats like brownies, cookies, and other sweets in opaque containers, rather than clear dishes.

Display healthy foods. Once you have squirreled away the high-fat, high-calorie foods, set out fruits, vegetables, and other healthy treats. Use glass bowls for rinsed grapes, or keep a teeming fruit basket on the counter next to the fridge. You may reconsider the ice cream if you see a fresh pear on the way to the freezer.

Serving Strategies

Table time is crunch time, when you are faced with all the fragrances and presentations of food. Your senses are flooded, and you want to dig in.

How can you enjoy your time at the table without falling prey to a strong impulse to eat and eat and eat?

Serve buffet-style. Instead of putting the pot or bowl on the table, dish out the food in the kitchen, then take your plate to the dining room to eat. If you want seconds, you have to go get the food, which allows you time to think twice.

Eat and run. This is not very polite, so I recommend doing it when you are eating alone or with very understanding loved ones. After you finish eating, excuse yourself quickly and put the temptation to continue the feeding frenzy behind you.

Let someone else cook. As cook, you know just how good this food is. After all, you made it and therefore earned a heaping helping, right? Plus, when you cook it's hard to resist "quality control" samples. Not cooking greatly reduces your contact with large amounts of food. What a great excuse to get out of work!

Fib to stop food pushers. You know the type: Constantly offering food, they just won't take no for an answer. If "no" won't work, fib. Say that the dish gives you gas, your doctor advised you against eating it, you're allergic to it, or you're full but will gladly take a helping home. Distract the food pushers with compliments about the dish and ask to write down the recipe.

Thought for Week 7

You do have a very effective recourse when someone in your family fails to support your exercise and weight management program. Consider this Chinese proverb: "If thy enemy wrongs thee, buy each of his children a drum." That might make them think twice about being less than encouraging!

11

Week 8 and Beyond: Walk On, You Athlete, You!

As we come into the eighth week of the program, I think it's a great time to talk about "false summits." During a recent climbing trip, my co-author, Gary Legwold, and his mountain climbing buddy knew they were near the top of California's Mt. Whitney, which, at 14,494 feet above sea level, is the highest point in the contiguous United States. A whiteout made visibility poor, so they could not see the summit.

The pair kept going, knowing they were close but not exactly how close. They followed the path and would spy what they hoped was the flattened area of the actual summit—only to discover upon reaching the area that the path kept going.

This false summit scene repeated itself for about 45 minutes. Each false summit raised their hopes and gave them energy for that final push. But each time they realized the push was not final, they were let down and became discouraged. They thought about quitting, and they wondered if somehow they had become lost. They became physically and emotionally

GOALS FOR WEEK 8:

• Mall walk seven times, 30 minutes each time

• Make two walks Power Walks: alternate 5 minutes of walking and 1 minute of exercising five times, for a total of 30 minutes

• Eat healthy while dining out

• Lose 2 pounds

exhausted, cursing the whiteout that prevented them from seeing the summit.

The two friends eventually reached the peak, but it wasn't until later, as they enjoyed a celebration dinner, that they realized their mistake. They would have done better just to keep going steadily one step at a time on the path and not be so focused on the summit. The summit, they came to understand, was rewarding but not the end. After all, there still was an exhausting trip back down the mountain. And because the experience was so challenging, rewarding, and fun, there were to be many other mountains they wanted to climb—a lifetime's worth.

I tell you my friend's story because you are in the final week of the WalkSport Fit Forever Program. You may have the feeling that you are near the "summit" and want to race ahead to be done. I will tell you, though, that the end of this week is a false summit.

You may reach a particular fitness or weight management goal, just as my friend finally made it to the top of Mt. Whitney. But, as my friend explains it, there is a significant difference between a mountain climber—one who enjoys the process and benefits of mountain climbing more than the peaks themselves—and a "peak bagger," who values the trophy summit more than the experience of getting there.

Please don't become a "peak bagger." Yes, I want you to reach your goals, your "summits," but they should only be part of the journey. More importantly, I want you to keep going steadily, a step at a time, on your way to good health. Take the opportunity to enjoy the process and benefits of exercise and weight management along the way.

This week, your goal is to lose 2 pounds, which means over the 8 weeks of my program your weight loss total will be 8 pounds. My guess is you have probably had a week (or two) when you lost 2 pounds—maybe more. I am confident that you're reaping the benefits of using your diary to do weekly meal planning and record all that you eat. Keep up the good work. With all the weight management tips and techniques in this book, you are probably gaining confidence that you can reach your weight management goals.

Concerning the weekly mall walking goals, you are most likely on a roll and feeling the improvements in your stamina and strength. Have you made any new mall walking friends? I bet your "dance card" is as full as you want it to be, and you and your friends are helping each other to better health.

To prepare you for your life beyond this program, we'll talk about avoiding overuse injuries, the benefits of hiring a personal trainer, and strategies for dining out—all strategies you can use to improve far into the future.

Avoiding Overuse Injuries

As you continue mall walking beyond these 8 weeks, you may want to increase your exercise time to 45 minutes or even an hour each day. Many people feel that once going, a half hour of mall walking flies by pretty quickly and they don't want to stop. I will warn you, however, that making this increase in exercise time all at once can lead to excessive fatigue, burnout, and injuries.

Let's take a moment to cover injuries associated with mall walking. I am happy to say that mall walking is largely an injury-free activity. If you watch joggers, you can understand why walking is comparatively easier on the body than running. Walkers transfer their body weight smoothly from one foot to the other, while joggers bound from foot to foot, transferring three to four times their body weight on the landing foot. That can add up to quite a pounding on the feet, ankles, knees, and back.

But as a mall walker, you're not immune to injuries, especially if you don't make a habit of warming up, stretching, and cooling down. Some walkers develop lower-back pain or fractures. Others have ankle sprains, blisters, and muscle soreness. Most mall walking injuries are from overuse. Let's look at four of the more common overuse injuries. (Rest and always see your doctor if you experience any of these injuries.)

Arch and heel pain. This is often plantar fasciitis, which is an inflammation of the band of tissue stretching from heel to toe. Pain may not be present while you walk, but it hobbles you upon rising in the morning and after a rest from walking. Chronic plantar fasciitis can lead to heel spurs. This condition is largely the result of poor arch support, so be sure your walking shoes are adequate. Also, avoid walking barefoot in your home. Consult the experienced staff in a specialized walking or running store for better information on the best shoes for you.

Shin pain. Muscle or tendon weakness in the front or inside of the lower leg may lead to sharp pains, often called shinsplints. This injury usually happens when people are unaccustomed to training, especially on hard surfaces such as mall floors, and when people increase their walking distance or speed too fast. As with plantar fasciitis, poor arch support is a major factor in shinsplints.

Achilles pain. This is a slow degeneration and weakening of the tendon between the calf and heel. Tight calf muscles, lack of warming up and stretching, too much walking on hard surfaces, and doing too many stairs can lead to Achilles tendinitis.

Knee pain. The most common overuse injury to the knee is chondromalacia patella, sometimes called walker's knee. The kneecap normally moves up and down in a groove as you bend and straighten your knee. If the kneecap is misaligned, it will pull off to one side and grate on the side of the groove and under the kneecap. This grating causes cartilage on the side of the groove and the back of the kneecap to wear out. You can also experience fluid buildup, swelling, and pain. The pain is especially strong after you have been sitting for a while. The problem stems from the foot, and good arch support helps prevent and heal the condition. This happens more often with women and it is worse when going up and down stairs.

Personal Trainer Benefits

As motivated as you were when you started, you may hit the wall in your mall walking and weight management program. A personal trainer can peel you off the wall, give you a different approach, and send you off with a pat on the back. If you're trying to reach a particular fitness goal and learn the latest training techniques, or if you've stopped your program and need a jump-start, you'll definitely benefit from a personal trainer's professional help.

Personal trainers help you toe the line, in a good way. One study put 20 men on a 12-week strength training program. Some worked out on their own, and others used a personal trainer. Those using the trainer had strength gains 30 to 45 percent greater than the men who did not have professional help—and they achieved their gains 30 percent faster.

You can hire a trainer for as little as $20 an hour. You may only need a few sessions with your trainer, who may be open to allowing you and a friend to do two-client sessions and split the cost. To find a personal trainer in your area, check the Yellow Pages, call health clubs, and con-

MALL WALKING MAVEN

Ernie Beat the Eating Out Challenge

My friend Ernie has used almost-daily mall walking to help him lose 30 pounds over the last 4 years or so. There have been two "casualties" in this process: his 17½ neck-size shirts (he now wears a 16) and dining out.

Ernie and his wife, Cathy, have not completely banned eating out, but they have cut back since they started watching what they eat. Ernie recently had a lapse, he says, because he had a work assignment that put him on the "rubber-chicken circuit," an affectionate term for the business banquet fare in many hotels. "Unfortunately, it makes it hard to diet as much as I'd like to," he says.

Buffet dining is especially tough, says Ernie, "because you eat entirely too much. I like those places, but after I eat there I have to make sure I walk it off or starve—and starving is no fun."

Ernie admits he and Cathy are now very picky about the social gatherings they attend. "I ask, 'What are you serving?' If it is a big dinner—like prime rib and cocktails and all that—we don't go unless we absolutely have to. If they are serving fish and salads, you know, something healthy, then maybe we'll go. But if we don't like the food, we decline and save ourselves $45."

You gotta admire Ernie's resolve.

tact these organizations: American Council on Exercise, (800) 825-3636; IDEA, Inc., (800) 999-4332, ext. 246; and the National Strength and Conditioning Association, (800) 815-6826.

How to Dine Out

Even if you've been curtailing your restaurant habits in favor of home-cooked low-fat meals, you can't avoid going out forever. Luckily, you *can* dine out without pigging out and look yourself in the mirror the next morning. Here are 30 ways you can stay true to your goals while enjoying yourself thoroughly.

- Before you leave home, review the portion sizes in chapter 2. Keep these portions in mind when ordering. You will surely pass on that 14-ounce steak if you remember that 3 to 4 ounces is considered to be a healthy portion for most people.

- Snack on an apple (or two) and a bit of cheese before going out to eat. This snack covers the magic sugar, starch, protein, and fat combo for satiety, so you won't enter the restaurant so ravenous.

- Have a friend call you on your cell phone before you walk into the restaurant. Ask her to coach you and remind you of how to order wisely.

- Read the nutrition guide at fast, food restaurants. Brace yourself for some whopping numbers, though. Use all that you know about fat grams and daily calorie requirements to choose your meal wisely, including saying no to "supersizing."

- Make one trip—out the door. If the menu is wrong and the management won't work with you to create a healthy meal, then just take your business elsewhere.

- Order a side dish of extra vegetables, grains, or fruits. You can fill up on these healthy foods and eat less meat and rich sauces.

- Ask that fatty sauces and salad dressings be served on the side. That way, you can have just enough of that great taste, but you won't have to worry about so many calories. You may also want to BYOD (bring your own dressing), a small bottle of a low-calorie brand that fits in your purse or pocket.

- Specify how you want food cooked. Some establishments will let you order grilled or broiled meats instead of fried, which has more fat and calories. Another example would be to order French toast made with egg whites only. As a rule, ask the waiter not only how your food is cooked, but also what ingredients are in a dish (and make sure to ask that the cook not brush the food with butter).

- Choose from the kids' or seniors' menu. Portions are smaller— and so is the cost.

- Order the "instead of" way, using the following table:

Instead of this . . .	Order this . . .
Caffe mocha	Coffee
Cream for coffee	Low-fat milk
Cream soups	Broth-based soups with lots of veggies
Salad dressing	Lemon wedges or gourmet vinegar
French fries	Baked potato, fruit, or a small green salad
Buttered vegetables	Fresh, steamed vegetables
Meat in gravy	Meat in its own juice
Cream sauce	Tomato sauce
Marinated in oil or butter	Marinated in juice or wine
Hard-shell tacos	Soft-shell tacos
Mayonnaise on sandwich	Mustard, lettuce, tomato, onion
Sweet and sour pork	Chicken chow mein
Fettuccine Alfredo	Spaghetti with marinara sauce
Beef chimichanga	Chicken fajitas
Prime rib	Filet mignon
Cheesecake	Angel food cake with strawberries
Danish	Small bagel with jelly
Croissants	French bread
Large popcorn, butter	Small popcorn, no butter

- Select your meals a la carte. You get exactly what you want by doing this. Full meals often give you more than you need. Yes, ordering a la carte can be more expensive, but not compared with the "cost" of extra pounds.

- Keep the waiter hopping, and keep your appetite in check, by drinking lots of water.

- Nurse your drink. Alcohol is loaded with calories, especially hard liquor and sweetened drinks. If you must, order one drink and make it last.

- Pass on appetizers and bread. I know you are excited about the wonderful meal coming, but save your eating for the big show, not the warmup act.

- Or eat *only* appetizers and bread. Both of these are usually very tasty and filling, so skip the main meal.

- Or use appetizers and bread as fillers. These will slow your hunger so you will eat less of the high-fat and high-calorie foods that make up the main meal—box up the rest of your main course for tomorrow's dinner.

- Make two trips to the salad bar. The first is for loading up on raw fruits and vegetables; the second is for small samplings of cole slaw, potato salad, pudding, and the rest of the higher fat temptations.

- Watch the salt. Restaurant food is typically salty, so ask about the milligrams of sodium in the food you order. You may want to call the restaurant manager, and discuss which dishes would be best to order. Federal government dietary guidelines recommend limiting your salt intake to 2,400 milligrams per day.

- Find the fiber. This nutrient, which is in breads, beans, pasta, fruits, and vegetables, helps control cholesterol and reduces the risk of heart disease. You should eat between 25 and 30 grams of fiber each day. Most fast foods have less than 3 grams, but a 7-ounce bean burrito has as much as 13 grams; a taco salad has 7.

- Settle for cereal. You may think that because you are eating at a restaurant, you have to get your money's worth by eating a lot of the restaurant's best fare. Shift your focus from the food you're having to the fun you're having with friends and family. When you go to your favorite waffle place, for instance, instead of having waffles—which with syrup and butter can come to 900 calories—have cereal, fruit, and an English muffin.

- Main dish restaurant portions are often huge, so order Chinese style. Make it a habit to get one fewer entrée than the number of people seated at your table, then divide and dig in. Bonus: You get a number of different tastes, instead of one big meal.

- When you order pizza, ask the pizza maker to make an extra-thick crust and go light on the cheese. Top the pie with veggies. Skip the pepperoni, sausage, Canadian bacon, or hamburger, which can be very high in fat, saturated fat and certain artificial additives.

- Skin your fried chicken. Just eat the meat, and avoid the high fat and extra calories in the fried skin. Try one nibble, if you must, but think of it as a french fry, not part of the chicken itself.

- Use a napkin to signal you're done. You don't have to finish all of that monstrous meal that many restaurants offer. Leave some food on your plate and cover it with your napkin. That is a sign for the waiter to remove the plate.

- Bring a bag. My friend Virginia always does this, just in case the restaurant doesn't have take-home containers. Then she automatically cuts her entrée in half and puts one portion in the bag. Better yet, have the waiter do it for you, then serve you half and let the other half cool in the kitchen for bagging later.

- "Order" your dessert at home. Decide on dessert before you are seated at the restaurant, where pie a la mode always looks particularly tempting. At home or the office, consult your diary and consider what you have eaten already and what you plan to eat. Can you afford the dessert calories today?

(continued on page 188)

MALL WALKING MAVEN

Stewart Walked Off 143 Pounds

Stewart is the memorable character I mentioned in chapter 1 who used mall walking to lose 114 pounds. He stands 6 feet 8½ inches, and about 5 years ago he weighed 346 pounds. He knew he needed to lose weight, and, as a bus driver, he knew he was not getting any on-the-job exercise. So on January 3, 1997, he resolved to walk, and he headed to a mall, an experience he found "scary." The size of the mall did not scare him as much as his fear of failure. "I wanted to have success," he says, "and taking that first step is always the hardest part." Stewart walked around the mall one time that day. During his 20 minutes of walking, Stewart met a few mall walkers, who were warm and friendly. They told him he would love mall walking.

They were right. His second week, Stewart walked twice around the mall. "One day when I was walking, this tall blonde wearing black leotards zoomed by me," recalls Stewart. "I'm competitive, and I said, 'Darn if I'm going to have a lady buzz by me.' So I tried to catch her as she flew around corners, but I didn't have the stamina."

The person Stewart was trying to catch that day was yours truly. We finally did meet, and I convinced him to join the mall walking club. "It was the best thing that ever happened to me," he says. He liked the support and the incentive programs the club offered. In 3 months he continued to mall walk and limit his calories to 2,000 a day, and he lost 50 pounds. I helped Stewart with his walking posture and speed, and I showed him how to swing his arms in a power-arm position. "I learned that dieters lose weight, but they also lose muscle tone," he says. "Mall walking helped me keep my tone."

By November of that year Stewart's pants size had dropped from 56 to 38. "I was so excited to go to Nordstrom and buy a pair of pants—the first I had purchased from anywhere other than a big-and-tall store."

The pounds kept rolling off, until Stewart's weight went down to 203—a loss of 143 pounds in 1½ years. However, he felt weak at that weight. When he came down with strep throat, his doctor said Stewart had lost too much weight too fast. Stewart started eating a bit more. He gained about 30 pounds and felt good at around 230 pounds.

A couple of years ago, an upstairs toilet broke in Stewart's house while he was away, and 46,000 gallons of water flowed freely until he returned. He and his family were forced to eat restaurant food for over 5 months. He would watch his portions (except veggies, which he freely piled on his plate), eat slowly, cut his food into small bites, eat only one slice of bread (no butter), avoid alcohol, and take half of the entrée home or not clean his plate, but still, he struggled to manage his weight. He would have slips but not be too hard on himself. "I figured you couldn't regain all the weight in one day," he says. "If I gained half a pound from the slip, I told myself that I could lose it again in a couple of days of walking."

Unfortunately, the stress of his housing situation wiped out Stewart's mall walking, and his weight climbed to 270. "One night at supper, my son said, 'Dad you need to walk more,'" says Stewart. "We decided it was time to go to our lake cabin to get away, to walk, and to eat home-cooked meals again. We had to carry water in, but it was worth it to prepare our own fresh vegetables and fruits, which are hard to get in restaurants." Stewart and his family started regularly walking the scenic roads around the lake.

All is relatively quiet on the home front now, and Stewart is back to home (read "healthy") cooking. His weight is dropping, and he is confident it will return to 230 pounds. He walks 5 days a week, sometimes around the neighborhood but usually at the mall.

"The other mall walkers, the staff, the security guards—they are all caring, friendly people who are great to be around," says Stewart. "The mall has become a part of my life.

"When I started mall walking, Sara was the gal I wanted to pass, or at least to be able to talk with and not be out of breath. Well, I can do that now. In fact, the other day I was walking outside and this jogger teased me about not being as fit as he. So I jogged with him until he tired out. Then I jogged home."

- If you blow it, enjoy it. Lapses happen. Relax, and then get back to mall walking and your normal healthy foods tomorrow. Some nutritionists advise their clients to follow the 80/20 Rule: Eat well 80 percent of the time and eat what you want 20 percent of the time. This rule gives you some wiggle room.

- Get up and dance. If you're at a restaurant that offers live music, grab a partner and cut a rug. It's good exercise, and you can't eat on the dance floor.

- Have a candlelight conversation. How can you stuff your face when your partner is sitting across the table looking so fine? Talk about the two of you, say sweet nothings, reminisce. Shift the focus away from the food, onto yourselves.

- Praise managers of restaurants that offer healthy foods—and make sure you bring others to dine there.

Well, you've done it—you've officially adopted the mall walking way of life. Don't look at this as the summit of the mountain—see it as one wonderful lookout onto the vista of your healthy life. When you're done patting yourself on the back, lace up those shoes and head for the mall for more fun and more exciting challenges. But first, check out chapter 14 to learn how to continue building on your success.

Thought for Week 8

"There will be a time when you believe everything is finished. That will be the beginning."

—Louis L'Amour

Part III

Mall Walking for SPECIAL People

Mall Walking during and after Pregnancy

During and after pregnancy, malls can be heavenlike to women who want a workout.

"That was especially true after I had my first baby," says Anne, who walked right through three pregnancies in 3 years. "At first it was great to be home with my son after having worked for so long. But everyone I knew was working, so it got kind of lonely. At the mall, I could connect with people and exercise. It was great."

When I am walking at the mall, I often see "mom brigades," groups of mothers who gather with friends to stroll in a safe, climate-controlled space. I have to laugh when I think about one young mother I met who explained how she came to mall walking. She was in the habit of taking her young son for stroller rides in the great outdoors. Guess what was one of the first words her son spoke? "Cold." (I'm sure it wasn't long before he was saying "mall.")

I see mothers come to the mall carrying babies in backpacks and "frontpacks." They graduate to strollers when the load becomes too heavy, and then to wagons when the load becomes too many. Not all those in the mom brigades are moms. I once watched a man, probably in his late twenties, as he pushed his baby in a stroller while reading a paperback. I remember thinking that he couldn't be getting much of a workout, so I struck up a conversation and got to know him a bit.

The father told me that his 3-month-old daughter, Kira, had been born with heart problems. She needed to be attached to a heart monitor and required almost constant attention. He was on paternity leave, and his wife had already exhausted her maternity leave. He said he had gained weight from all the Kira-sitting and supervising, but when he heard about mall walking, he began strolling with Kira. He told me he'd lost 25 pounds (and I thought he wasn't getting much of a workout!), and Kira clearly enjoyed the sights and sounds of the mall during their 1-hour to 2-hour strolls.

Mall Walking and Pregnancy

I applaud pregnant moms who mall walk, for their determination and resourcefulness. It's very inspiring to be around people who really want to walk—you can't hold them back. From my own experience, I have always known that mothers-to-be are keen about being in their bodies during the special time of pregnancy. Pregnant moms are protective of the fetuses they carry, and they use their intellect, common sense, and instincts to not only avoid doing harm to the unborn baby, but to also do the baby—and themselves—some good. They also want to keep their shape and make the delivery as smooth as possible, so they walk.

In all three of her pregnancies, Anne walked right up to the day before delivery.

"I had fast and easy labors and deliveries, and the doctor said the fact that I had walked regularly and kept in good shape probably helped," she says. "I also feel that it helped with water retention. Walking sort of helped keep the fluids flowing inside me. I know I had more of a problem with water retention with my first one because I worked at a desk then, and the only time I had to walk was a little at lunchtime."

Doctors and midwives agree that moderate exercise such as mall walking during pregnancy can benefit the mother and does not appear to interfere with oxygen delivery to the fetus. Obviously, you should consult with your doctor first. But in most cases, doctors are happy to see mothers-to-be start moderate walking during pregnancy if they have not walked previously, or continue to walk if they have.

According to the American College of Obstetricians and Gynecologists (ACOG), "regular exercise improves a woman's physical and mental health at a time when she may feel tired, overweight, and moody." ACOG also says exercising and being fit may improve a woman's ability to handle labor pain and to get back in shape after the baby is born.

Doctors and midwives have several safety concerns about pregnant women who exercise, and, again, I emphasize that you should continually check with your doctor as you exercise during pregnancy. Doctors do not want pregnant women to do jarring exercises, high-intensity activities that elevate heart rates and body temperatures, or exercises requiring sudden or deep-squatting movements. Doctors are slow to give the green light to exercise for pregnant women with histories of miscarriage, multiple pregnancy, or premature dilation; who are too headstrong to set exercise limits during pregnancy; or who limit their food and fluid intake for dieting reasons.

That said, moderate exercise offers many benefits during pregnancy. Exercise helps you be more energetic because it maintains your cardiorespiratory system and your stamina. Walking is easy on joints, which is important, because during pregnancy hormones cause a loosening of joints to allow the baby's head to pass through the pelvic area. In contrast, more jarring exercise can lead to injuries. Walking also maintains your muscle tone and strength, and therefore helps you carry the extra weight of the fetus. Finally, as a walker, you reduce the risk of varicose veins and leg cramps, and you maintain or improve your balance and coordination. In order to make the most of your mall walking during pregnancy, I offer the following suggestions:

Read. Ask you doctor or midwife for a list of recommended readings. One in particular that is often recommended is *Pregnancy and Exercise* by Raul Artal and G. S. Sharpe.

Eat, and eat some more. Drop the word "diet" from your vocabulary while you are pregnant, especially if you walk during pregnancy.

You need to eat extra to meet the needs of your unborn child and growing body. Check with your doctor about how much more you should eat, but often doctors recommend eating an extra 300 calories a day per fetus. Your doctor may require you to consume even more if you walk and do not experience the expected weight gains.

Drink up. Monitor your body temperature to make sure you don't overheat while mall walking. High body temperatures can cause birth defects. It is helpful that malls are climate controlled, so high heat and humidity outside should not be a factor, but hydration is. Drink 16 ounces of water before you start mall walking, and do not pass a single fountain without stopping for more water. Carry your own bottle and empty that as well. Do whatever it takes to stay hydrated. Also, wear lightweight and loose-fitting clothing that allows body heat to dissipate, and stop exercising the moment you feel feverish or begin to overheat.

Chill. Cool it with trying to be super fit. It's just not going to happen because, in this special state of pregnancy, your body won't perform as it normally does, and it needs special care. Your heart, lungs, and most of your body systems are doing double duty trying to supply oxygen and nutrients to you and the developing fetus. So don't strive for walking at the same intensities as before pregnancy. Also don't overstride; this can strain the hip joints and lower back, which are already straining under the new load of the fetus. Walk normally and increase your pace by taking more steps, not longer strides.

Don't Power Walk. Just plain old walking is enough during pregnancy. Put a hold on the Power Walking exercises until after the baby arrives.

Stretch gently. Do your pre- and postwalking stretching slowly and gently. Don't expect to have the same range of motion in your stretches as you did before your pregnancy.

Keep checking your pulse. You don't want intensity during this time, and the target heart rate zones no longer apply. Regularly check your pulse to make sure it's no higher than 140. If you can't talk while you walk, you're going too fast.

Change shoes and bra. You may have to wear shoes one-half to one size larger to allow room for foot swelling. Starting in the second trimester, you may want to wear a sports bra with wide shoulder straps. This provides good support, helps protect your breasts, and can prevent shoulder strain.

Expect some fatigue and discomfort. Some days you just won't have it. Try not to get frustrated. Walk a little and see if walking may actually help, but don't push it. Slight discomfort in your feet, legs, and the pelvic area is common, and when your belly starts to grow, your back may ache. Expect these kinds of aches, but stop walking and see your doctor if you have abdominal or chest pain, vaginal bleeding, severe breathlessness, a heart beat above 140, headache, dizziness, nausea, or if you are overheating.

Mall Walking through the Stages

Just as your body, and your baby's body, changes with each stage of pregnancy, your mall walking should change as well. Here's a brief overview of what to expect as you walk through the stages.

First trimester. This is a time of "downshifting," of changing your thinking about intensity especially. (If you're struggling with this one, reread "Chill" above). Morning sickness and fatigue may affect you. Again, walk a little to see if walking helps, but don't push it. If you are a mall walker already, continue doing what you have been doing. If you are starting to mall walk, use my program but don't do the Power Walk exercises. Do your warmups, stretching, and cooldowns, gently and slowly.

Second trimester. For some women, this time is a relatively comfortable, energetic interlude between the first and third trimesters. Keep mall walking, but by the 5th or 6th month you will notice that you are slowing down. Also, doctors advise not doing any exercise on your back starting in the second trimester. In this position, cardiac output is decreased in most pregnant women, which means less blood flow to the fetus. (Obviously, you are not on your back while mall walking, but you should know this in case you find yourself doing other exercises or household chores in this position.)

Third trimester. How slow can you go? You may be asking this question near the end of your pregnancy, because you are big and often huffing and puffing. Gentle walking can help give you energy, so if you feel like you want to stay with your program, do it. Anne did it, remember, right up to the day before she delivered each of her three babies. Take it easy, though. Always be aware of your body and take special care that you're not overexerting yourself.

Postpartum. You may be mall walking again a week or so after giving birth, but Anne says it took her 2 to 3 weeks to get back on her feet again and start walking. Check with your doctor about when to start mall walking again. Your body has been through a lot, you may be dealing with some postpartum depression, and, with a new one to care for, sleep can be in short supply.

Doctors say that it may take 6 to 9 months before you can get back to the kind of shape you were in before pregnancy. Go slowly, of course. You can always go through my mall walking program again. Remember, you start slow with my program, but you have success, which is always important. (Note: Nursing mothers need to drink plenty of water, and I'm sure would be very appreciative of the abundance of mall restrooms and water fountains.)

Family Time at the Mall

As a new mother, one of your challenges is having enough time—for sleep, family, work, and exercise. You may feel something has to give, and you may choose exercise. I understand your thinking, but let's see if we can make mall walking work. After all, you will need breaks, and mall walking will enhance your physical and emotional health. The way I see it, you have at least five options for getting some support.

1. **Dad can help.** In fact, Dad may get upset if he doesn't have alone time with the baby. Use that time to head to the mall.

2. **Mom and Dad can help.** We're talking about your parents, in-laws, aunts, uncles, and siblings. A little warning, though: This can get to be political with everyone wanting to take care of that cute baby. Set up a schedule so that everyone gets a fair share of baby time.

3. **Friends and neighbors can help.** You can take turns watching kids, and head to the mall when you are free. Set up a schedule and then make sure you respect the agreed-upon start and end times.

4. **Babysitters can help.** Paying someone for even an hour can do wonders for your attitude.

5. **Your children can help.** Use a backpack or stroller, and then double stroller or wagon. Shari meets her mom every day at the mall at 7 A.M. She carries her youngest and pulls her older two in a wagon as she walks and talks with her mom for an hour. "If I wasn't walking with her, I'd be on the phone for an hour with her anyway," says Shari. "I put the kids in the wagon with cereal, a tape player, and books, and off we go—four times around the mall. And we really go; we don't stop and chat that much. My legs and stomach are definitely tighter, and I can tell I'm getting stronger pulling that wagon."

While these morning times are workouts for Shari and her mom, Shari says she looks at them as an outing. "It's fun to see three generations of the family exercising and doing something together," she says. "I also like it that I am setting a good example for my kids. They know that in the morning we need to go to the mall for walking, and then we can go play."

This scene gives me a motivational idea to add to the list of 29 I provided at the end of chapter 3. Here's the idea: Ask your parents or grandparents to meet you at the mall for walks. As you walk together, ask if you can use a tape recorder to document their life story. The time will fly, the memories will be sweet and poignant, and at the end of the one or two (or more) walks that you will need to cover their life, you will have an heirloom on tape.

Anne remembers fondly meeting her parents for three-generation walks at the mall. Because her children are now in school, Anne is walking with a friend or by herself. But she thoroughly enjoyed the times that the six of them walked together.

"We'd meet every day, Monday through Friday at 8:30 A.M.," she says. "Grandpa would take one stroller, and I would take the other. At the time, they were changing the mall quite a bit, so there was always something new for the kids to look at. Plus it wasn't cold like it was outside. We'd walk 3 miles and then stop for a snack. It was great."

Anne found the mall to be a perfect place for exercise. She knew they were not going to get rained out. If something went wrong or if the kids started fussing and screaming, there would always be someone passing by who understood and offered a helping hand.

Like Shari, Anne feels it is important to set an example for her children. "For them to learn to eat right and make exercise part of a daily routine is very important. I felt I was not only telling them to exercise but also doing it. And they have remembered that. They are now active in exercise and sports, and they ask me regularly if I got out and exercised that day. They're checking on me," she smiles.

Following in Your Footsteps

Funny how this mall walking community just keeps going and growing. How many times have we heard mall walkers in this book say they keep at their program because their other mall walking friends are, like Anne's children, "checking" on them? This community support, the buddy system, getting by with a little help from my friends—call it whatever you want—is indeed a powerful agent for change. It is especially powerful as it passes from one generation to another within the family.

Too often, when adults join a fitness program, they leave their kids home on the couch. In certain cases, this is understandable—not many 3-year-olds want to (or could) join Mommy for a 5-mile run. That's not the case with mall walking, as we have seen with the families of Shari and Anne. Just as their little ones learn from their parent's example about how important it is to brush their teeth every morning, they also learn how important it is to exercise each day.

As parents, we can sometimes get by with just telling our kids to do something. But we have a better chance if we become role models and *show* them. It is our unspoken messages—our concrete actions—that often make a more lasting impression on our kids than the things we say. Parents are vital role models when it comes to exercise. Studies have shown that children of physically active moms are twice as likely to be active as children of inactive moms. Children of active dads are 3½ times more likely to be active as children of inactive dads. And in families where both parents are physically active, children are nearly six times more likely to be involved in an exercise program later in life than kids whose parents do not keep fit.

I see two strengths in families using my program to do mall walking together: First, it helps a family define fitness and good nutrition as important and fun; second, it encourages families to do healthy things together, to walk side-by-side and in doing so, develop and deepen a special intimacy that is theirs alone.

Launching the Young Ones

I've read many troubling news reports about the fitness of our youth. The reports often boil down to this: TV, computers, video games, junk food, and lack of exercise are making our children fat and unhealthy. One study says that childhood obesity in our country is at an all-time high, and 40 percent of children between ages 5 and 8 are obese, have elevated blood pressure and cholesterol, and are not active. Other studies find that more than 80 percent of obese adolescents become obese adults, and only one-fifth of adolescents diagnosed with obesity receive treatment for it.

As a parent, you want to do whatever you can to get your children going on the right track with fitness. Here are 35 ways to support your child's interest in exercise and health.

- Make yourself available for family fitness outings, such as mall walking workouts, bicycling and canoeing trips, golf games, roller skating, sledding and skiing fun, Frisbee games, swimming and playground times, and more.

- Plan active vacations that include hiking, biking, tennis, golf, or skiing.

- Play jump-roping games with your child. Don't worry, your child will teach you how!

- Play tag, hide-and-seek, hopscotch, and other children's games that involve running and movement.

- Ask your child to join you for exercise. Take a soccer ball with you on family picnics, and plan time to kick the ball around with your family.

- Buy an aerobics video and ask your child to join in as you follow the tape. Or enroll in a parent-child aerobics class at a health club.

- Take a martial arts class together as a family. Typically, classes offer achievement goals shared by the family, a great workout, increased discipline, and confidence concerning self-defense.

- Walk to the local library, video store, or coffee shop instead of driving, and take your child with you.

- Encourage your child to participate in sports.

- If you know your child is interested in a particular sport, watch a high school, college, or professional game, or go to a 10-K, marathon, hall of fame museum, or movie about the sport.

- Budget money to fund your child's participation on sports teams and the purchase of sports equipment.

- Give gear and equipment such as a baseball glove, basketball, or sports shoes to your child as birthday and holiday gifts.

- Attend your child's games, and discuss her progress.

- Volunteer to coach your child's sports team, and work with him at home on skills.

- Play in an adult softball, volleyball, basketball, or hockey league yourself and ask your child to come to your games.

- Limit the amount of time your child watches TV, is on the computer, and plays video games. (Instead, have them wear a step counter!)

- Limit the amount of time *you* watch TV, are on the computer, and play video games.

- Make a rule of no snacking while watching TV.

- Ask for your child's input when you develop your weekly meal plan. Let him help you make choices.

- Take your child along when you go to the grocery store, explaining the food choices you make.

- Teach your child to read food labels, and then send her on a "treasure hunt" in the grocery store, looking for the cereal with the least amount of sugar or the munchies with the least amount of fat.

- Keep healthy foods, especially snacks, in the home.

- Take a healthy-cooking class and then show off your new skills and recipes to your family.

- Purchase good cutlery, pots and pans, and other cooking equipment so that you and your child can easily prepare healthy meals.

- Ask your child to help prepare meals, and explain the importance of sensible portion sizes and of eating a variety of foods.

- Buy your child a kid's cookbook and say, "You are responsible for Tuesday's dinner." Then eat the meal and praise your child's healthy food choices.

- Minimize the use of food to reward or to quiet your child.

- Make breakfast a must, and then join your family for this most important meal.

- Encourage your child to enroll in physical education classes (if it is not required), and discuss what she is learning in class.

- Encourage your child to enroll in a nutrition class, and discuss what he is learning in class.

- At teacher conferences, ask how much physical activity your child receives during the school day. Also ask to see the nutritional information for the school lunch menus, and send a bag lunch with your child if the school lunch is unsatisfactory.

- Talk with the school principal about removing vending machines or limiting students' access to them.

- Take your child along when you go to the doctor, explaining your health concerns and the importance of regular checkups and taking care of your body.

- Get 8 hours of sleep, and make sure your child gets at least that amount.

- Stop smoking.

You can probably think of several more ways to support your child's interest in exercise and health. Use the same creativity that Shari and Anne used in finding a way to make this fun and rewarding for everyone. Developing this interest and motivating your children takes time, but I don't know of a better investment in your child's future health.

13

Arthritis Relief at the Mall

One June day a few years ago, I had pain so pervasive I thought I would lose my mind. All of my joints suddenly ached with an intensity that had me frantic for relief. It had started with a nagging feeling that no matter what I did I just couldn't seem to get comfortable. It worsened to the point that I hobbled to the bathtub and filled it with water as high as it would go. I was desperate to become buoyant and take the pressure off my joints.

As it turned out, I was lucky, if you call lucky getting a nasty case of the flu. My condition was blessedly short in duration, and I knew it would pass in a day or two. But the episode made me think about people who have to endure arthritis and other chronic painful conditions. As I watched the bathtub fill with hot water, I thought that this is what many of their days must be like.

As I walk in malls all around the country, I talk with people who appear to be ordinary mall walkers like the rest of us. But they are not. They have arthritis and are heroes of mine. They struggle to get up from bed, to get dressed, to get out the door and to the mall—actions the rest of us take for granted—then they proceed to walk right through pain.

How Do You Spell Relief? W-A-L-K

Arthritis refers to more than 100 different diseases, including osteoarthritis, fibromyalgia, rheumatoid arthritis, gout, spondylarthropathies, juvenile arthritis, juvenile rheumatoid arthritis, and lupus. Arthritis mostly affects areas in and around joints, although the disease also can affect other parts of the body. It causes pain, loss of movement, and sometimes swelling.

When you look at those symptoms of arthritis, you could easily conclude that people with arthritis don't exercise. That was true about 20 years ago, but not now. Not only do they exercise, they do it longer than people who don't have arthritis. According to research, 75 to 85 percent of people with arthritis who begin an exercise program are likely to stick with it for 4 years. That exercise adherence rate is close to twice as high as the average American's.

Arthritis experts say people with arthritis are so good about exercising for one very important reason—they feel relief. People who exercise because they have high blood pressure, heart problems, or want to lose weight *know* that it is good to exercise, but people with arthritis *feel* that it is good to exercise. When they walk, they experience relief from pain. That positive reinforcement keeps them going.

Here's another point: Exercise builds confidence that you can self-manage arthritis. That confidence comes from knowing you are strong in spite of the disease, capable of moving smoothly without straining the joints, and that your muscles absorb shock to your joints. The more you exercise, the more you believe in your ability to live a full, rich life despite the arthritis.

In the last 20 years, the list of benefits of exercise for arthritis has grown, but you could condense the list and say exercise helps to:

- **Prevent premature death.** Many people with arthritis are inactive and unfit, factors contributing to coronary heart disease, high blood pressure, diabetes, strokes, and certain kinds of cancer. You may not die of arthritis, but it can limit your lifestyle and lead to fatal conditions.

- **Prevent disability.** Appropriate rest helps reduce joint inflammation, but excessive rest weakens and atrophies muscles, tendons, ligaments, and bones; reduces joint range of motion; degenerates joint cartilage; and causes loss of endurance. These changes cause pain that is separate from arthritis pain but nevertheless contributes to disability.

- **Relieve discomfort and despair.** Appropriate exercise, such as mall walking, can alleviate joint stiffness and pain. Studies show that people with arthritis who are faithful exercisers have enhanced sleep and self-esteem, and they suffer less from stress, anxiety, and depression.

- **Reduce costs.** Medications and medical treatments are only part of the cost of arthritis. A more significant cost is related to disability, which can lead to lost earnings and, in many instances, forfeiture of health insurance benefits. Exercise helps reduce disability and costs.

Today, most doctors recommend mall walking or some other form of low-impact exercise for people with arthritis. And why wouldn't they, considering these benefits and the fact that exercise can improve an arthritic person's ability to do daily activities, a pretty impressive benefit all by itself? Well, over the last 2 decades there have been concerns that exercise may accelerate the development of arthritis.

Good news: Research on runners, whose joints take far more pounding than mall walkers, shows that this is not the case. One study of 50- to 72-year-old long distance runners showed that, compared with average members of the community, the runners had less physical disability, functioned better in daily activities, sought medical services less often, and continued to weigh less as they aged. A 5-year study of runners aged 50 and older showed no differences between the runners and nonrunners in the development of worn joints or arthritis.

Doctors have not always been so enthusiastic about exercise in the

Peg Overcame Arthritis

Peg, a 76-year-old mall walking friend of mine, remembers a dancer acquaintance who developed arthritis 40 years ago. Doctors banned him from the stage and told him to rest—with disastrous results. One can only imagine what bed rest did to the dancer's soul, but it disabled his body, to be sure. "He was pushed in a wheelchair, and his legs would stick out straight," she recalls. "I think that guy would have been better off had he kept moving and dancing, because he was stiff as a board."

Peg developed scoliosis when she was 12. She says all her growth went to one side of her body and she had to wear a brace that prevented her from growing only on one side. Women in her family are nearly 6 feet tall, yet, because of the brace and the scoliosis, she is 5 feet 1 inch tall. She has four curves in her spine, a hump on the right side of her back, and one leg shorter than the other. She has worn a lift in her shoe to correct for the shorter leg.

Peg did not let the scoliosis stop her from enjoying life. She married and worked, most recently in the K-Mart jewelry department until she retired. She has always been a very active worker with her church. "I overdo it," she says. "I will work at the church rummage sale, on hard floors, from 9 A.M. to 9 P.M. Or I will get to vacuuming and doing housework, and the day gets away from me. I don't know when to quit."

About 10 years ago, Peg started noticing some pain in the hip and knee

treatment of arthritis. In fact, doctors used to advise rest and absolutely no exercise for arthritis. The prevailing wisdom at the time was "if it hurts to move, do not move any more than you have to."

Now, exercise doesn't cure arthritis. Just because you mall walk does not mean you won't have problems opening jars or car doors. You will of her shorter leg. She didn't bother with it, because it wasn't enough to slow her down. "And I'm not really a doctor person," she admits.

However, in the last 4 or 5 years the pain worsened to the point where she could not bend to tie her shoes. The pain, stiffness, and fatigue increased when the weather was cold, damp, snowy, and blustery. "It scared me," says Peg, who finally went to her doctor. His diagnosis: arthritis.

At that point the liability of not knowing when to quit became an asset. Peg started walking, even though she had not been much for exercise until then. "I sort of thought it was foolish at my age," she admits. "But so many friends my age, they just sit there in their houses, don't walk, and then give me some good-natured teasing about always being on the go."

Peg and her sister-in-law mall walked a few times a week and water-walked twice a week.

"I noticed a terrific difference in my arthritis," she says. "I do not walk fast because of my problem, but I do 1 continuous hour and then have coffee. It's really great. The mall is warm, clean, and filled with friendly people. I'm a widow and I live alone, so to see people and chat and walk is wonderful. I can do nothing but sing praises about mall walking.

"If I weren't walking," says Peg, "I'd probably be hurting more and complaining a lot. In the morning when I'm getting ready to go, I do feel pain. Then we'll go to the mall and I'll tell my sister-in-law, 'We have to get going. I'm hurting too much.' If I keep moving, things loosen up until I can go pretty good. Walking keeps the pain away."

still have flare-ups. Your response is simply to pull back from exercise for a while. Even with the pullbacks, though, you will want to keep exercising because it will help you sleep well, your muscles will be stronger, and your joints will work better. In a nutshell, it feels better to be able to feel better.

Sorting Pain

People with arthritis often cannot get past the idea of increased pain associated with increased physical activity. Perhaps you are turned off by the "no pain, no gain" notion that we talked about earlier, that has long plagued the fitness world. Or maybe it's because exercise can make you sore, at least initially, and you lump all pains together. Arthritis experts say this is common, that people with the disease confuse any kind of pain with the pain of arthritis. These people tell doctors, for example, that they have arthritis pain in their calf. The doctor replies that there is no joint in the calf, so the pain cannot be from arthritis.

Not all pain is the same. Doctors encourage patients to distinguish the pain of arthritis—which people with arthritis know so well—from the pain caused by inactivity. This pain is from joint immobility, general weakness, and muscle and tendon tightness—not a disease. Once people with arthritis start to exercise, the typical muscle soreness they feel after a workout has nothing to do with arthritis.

The point is this: Exercise, in the long run, usually helps *reduce* arthritis pain, not aggravate it. Experts say there are dangers associated with exercise—doing too much too soon, for example—but the most dangerous thing, considering all the benefits, is not exercising.

Getting Started

Your first move, of course, is to talk about exercise with your doctor, physical therapist, or occupational therapist. Get his or her advice and approval. These professionals can help you sort out one pain from another and advise you on exercising safely.

Then it's time to begin the WalkSport Fit Forever Program. Just try it for a week, and see how it goes. This may not seem like much, but making it through a week of exercise is a major accomplishment. You may just find out that you can do the exercise, work through the pain, and take an active role in managing your arthritis.

I also recommend contacting your local chapter of the Arthritis Foundation. Ask about their PACE program (People with Arthritis Can Exercise), which uses gentle activities to increase joint flexibility, range of motion, muscle strength, and overall stamina. To learn more about PACE, write to the Arthritis Foundation at 1330 West Peachtree Street, Atlanta, GA 30309. Or call (800) 283-7800 or visit www.arthritis.org.

Once you get through the first week of my program, go on to the second. You might as well. You made it through that first week and the second is a piece of cake. If you miss a workout or have a flare-up that sets you back, don't get discouraged. You may have overdone it initially, which can be looked at as a sign of your enthusiasm for exercise. Rest, but stick with it, decreasing next time the time and intensity of the exercise you do. Doctors tell patients that exercise may not be pain-free, but you should not have more pain 2 hours after exercise than you did before you started.

If you make it through 2 weeks of my program, then keep going through all 8. Consult with your doctor and make adjustments as you go. A few of the Power Walk exercises may be too much—if so, just don't do them. Modify, but keep mall walking. Above all, tailor your plan to you—and keep it fun!

- Think about the time of day when you are at your best, and plan to mall walk then.

- Wear comfortable workout clothes and shoes that provide good support.

- Warm up before you begin each workout, so that you are not exercising cold joints. Try stretching and doing range-of-motion exercises in a warm shower as a way of becoming loose. Or apply a heating pad or hot pack to the sore area.

- If you have a single inflamed joint, think creatively about how you can protect the joint and still exercise other joints and muscles.

- As you mall walk, focus on proper technique and form, which increases your enjoyment and decreases your risk of injury and pain.

- To cool down, slow your pace near the end of the mall walk. Gently stretch muscles you have used and ice sore areas.

Sticking With It

As you continue to mall walk, you may find your motivation occasionally wanes. The excuses will come: too tired, too busy, too bored. It happens. To counteract this, set goals and reread the motivational tips in chapter 3. I think it is especially helpful to mall walk with a friend who also has arthritis, or to join a health club class that is specifically for people with arthritis. The social aspect will keep you going, and the exchange of support between you and your buddies will help your commitment.

Obviously, I am partial to mall walking, yet I acknowledge that you may want to do a variety of activities that you enjoy. That's great, as long as this variety helps you keep going. Remember, however, that these activities should not replace range-of-motion exercises prescribed by your doctor. Choose more than one activity so you can vary workouts and avoid doing the same old same old. Mall walking is excellent, as is biking, low-impact aerobics, and gentle martial arts such as t'ai chi. While many people with arthritis eventually become joggers, beginners should avoid such high-impact activities.

Mall walker Peg will tell you that water activities are also ideal. Water provides buoyancy and lessens pressure on the joints. Water aerobics, swimming, and moving limbs through range-of-motion exercises in the water are great. You can use paddles and swim fins to increase resistance and strengthen muscles. As good as water activities are, however, doctors advise against limiting yourself to the water. You still need to do weight-bearing exercises at least twice a week in addition to your water workouts. Exercising on land keeps your bones strong and helps fight osteoporosis.

Many doctors recommend that people with arthritis do strength training at least twice a week. The Power Walk exercises in my program are a good start. Talk with your doctor about these exercises. Most of the Power Walk exercises are isotonic, meaning you move your joints to strengthen muscles. Beginners should start slowly—just move the joints without holding weights, then gradually progress to light weights. If you don't have dumbbells, use orange juice cans filled with rice, 1- or 2-pound bags of beans, or cans of soup.

Instead of having you do isotonics, doctors may suggest isometric strength exercises. These strengthen your muscles without joint movement, which can eliminate pain in many situations. Your doctor, physical therapist, or occupational therapist can show you many kinds of isometric exercises. Here is one example:

To strengthen thigh muscles, sit in a chair and cross your ankles. Push forward with your back leg and press backward with your front leg. Exert pressure evenly so your legs don't move. Hold for a 10 count, relax, then switch your leg position and repeat.

Careful instruction is needed with strength training, so work closely with your physical therapist, occupational therapist, and doctor. Let them advise you on the proper position and weight load for each strength-training exercise you do. Do not simply buy a set of weights and go home for a workout.

Kitchen Tips for Arthritis Relief

Preparing food is harder when pain, fatigue, and depression decrease the appetite of people with arthritis. Or they may have an appetite but lack the mobility or manual dexterity to make meals that require time and effort to prepare. To make food preparation easier, follow these tips from the Arthritis Foundation.

- Plan rest breaks during meal preparation time.
- Use good posture to avoid fatigue or strain while performing kitchen tasks.
- Arrange your kitchen for maximum convenience; keep utensils you use most where they are easy to reach. Move frequently used items to eye level. Install shelves that slide out and turntables for easy access to spices and other items.

- When grocery shopping, look for healthful "convenience" foods like fresh presliced or chopped vegetables from the supermarket produce department.

- Add fresh fruit and bread to a frozen dinner to make a complete, satisfying meal.

- Use labor-saving kitchen gadgets and appliances, such as electric can openers and microwave ovens, to make cooking tasks easier.

- Let dishes soak. You don't have to have them done right after dinner. Let them soak overnight so you don't have to scrub so hard. Also, it is nice to limber up the hands in the morning by working them in warm water.

- Replace heavy dishes. Use plastic or lightweight dishes instead.

- Buy flip-top bottles. It makes it easier to dispense dishwashing soap.

These tips help you get the job done, and they help keep your spirits up. What can be most frustrating with arthritis is feeling that you're at the whim of your condition. It was not that long ago that the best you could do for arthritis was sit and take it, and take your medicine. Now, doctors are advising the nearly 43 million Americans with arthritis or related conditions to get up and go. Go walk at the mall, go bike, go swim, go to the gym. Make sure to take plenty of precautions and take your arthritis medicine as well, but just keep going!

14

Taking the Next Step

I ran into my friend Conrad at the mall the other day. He had just finished another fine mall walking workout and felt pretty good about it.

"I'm going to have to eat off all this exercise," he quipped.

I laughed and thought about how far Conrad and other mall
walkers, including I, have come. Instead of complaining about having
to walk off all this food, at times we are almost gloating about having
to "eat off all this exercise." And now, you've joined a good group.
We're where we want to be in terms of fitness and weight management,
or at least we're headed in the right direction. And that gives us tremendous satisfaction and confidence. We can do this!

Begin Your Maintenance Plan

Note that I say, "We can do this!" as opposed to "We did it!" You may
have completed the WalkSport Fit Forever Program, lost 8 pounds—or
more—in 8 weeks, and are now as fit as you've ever been. Congratulations—you should feel great about what you did. My hope is that you
keep feeling great, day after day. This is only the beginning.

No doubt, you'll have to keep doing a fitness and weight management
program, unless you want to regain all the weight you lost. Typically,

weight loss programs produce average losses of 20 to 30 pounds over 12 to 20 weeks. Some people going through programs lose more, others lose less. Those results are good, but maintenance results are typically bad, because people quit doing their programs. At this point, it's almost a cliché—so many people go through big lifestyle conversions to lose weight, only to then backslide and regain the pounds.

Research finds this cliché to be true. One study found of the 152 men and women who participated in a 15-week exercise, behavior modification, and weight loss program, over the following 4 years less than 3 percent kept off the weight they had lost while in the program. Another study found 1-year weight loss results were impressive among 76 obese women, but 5 years after completing the weight loss program, only 5 percent maintained all of their weight loss.

It seems clear that weight loss, while not easy, is only the warmup act to the main event: maintenance—keeping your weight stable, either at a certain number of pounds or in a weight range. Researchers trying to pinpoint why maintenance fails for so many have determined that weight regain is related to genetic factors that cause the body to retain fat, the body's tendency to cling to fat reserves, and the buckling of wills in the face of family or social pressures.

Studies show people succeed at maintenance, on the other hand, when they feel in control of their eating habits. Successful people tended to experience initial success at weight loss, kept up an exercise program, used behavioral techniques taught in the studies, and ate fewer high-fat foods. Based on these results, here are 15 guidelines to help you succeed at maintenance.

Determine how much is enough. To maintain your weight, you need to establish a weight goal. For some reason, many people feel obligated to pick a big, round number like 50 or 100 pounds. Others set unrealistic goals based on comparisons to models, athletes, or movie stars. Instead, think about the times in your adult life you really felt good and what you weighed at that time. Also, make a list of friends and family members who are about your age and body build and who seem to be managing their weight well. What do these people weigh? These kinds of questions and reflections will give you a pretty good idea of the body weight you want to maintain.

Keep doing the food diary and your weekly meal plans. This kind of record keeping will keep you on track and help with maintenance. For example, you may believe that you are eating the right number of servings of fruit, but when you check your diary over the course of a week, you find out that you are not. You can prevent this kind of slip from becoming a big slide if you keep using your food diary. Schedule a regular time, like 15 minutes on Saturday morning, to review the previous week and plan for the next.

Control portion size. You don't have to cut out the most calorie-dense and tasty foods; just cut down. Deprivation, over the long haul, is the downfall of many maintenance programs. Don't become a restrained eater, because sooner or later you'll bust out of those restraints and become an omnivore on a mission—only to regret it later. By controlling portion sizes, you get to have enough of that cheesecake to say that you did it, without having to admit later that you *overdid* it. You not only get enough of a taste of your favorite foods, but you also get the confidence that you have control over what you eat.

Keep the focus on fat. I think of Lois and Donna when I think about focusing on fat. They both lost a tremendous amount of weight by making simple substitutions initially, like mustard for mayo on their sandwiches. Once they had their eyes opened as to how to make these kinds of substitutions over the course of eating three meals and a few snacks per day, they got on a roll and shed the pounds. The problem comes when you lose that focus and find fat again—back on your body, as Donna did. To do maintenance well, keep the focus on the fat in your food.

Eat a good breakfast. Many people who start slipping during maintenance stopped eating breakfast. Keep eating that all-important first meal of the day. Eating breakfast—even a small one—sets the tone for the rest of the day, helps distribute calories more evenly over three main meals, and activates a sleepy metabolism.

Carry a relapse prevention card. In maintenance, you are going to have lapses, temporary slips when you regain some weight but retain the determination to stick with your program. A *relapse*, on the other hand, is a loss of will; you call it quits and see yourself as a failure. To prevent a relapse, carry a card in your wallet or purse listing your high-risk foods and situations—and then avoid them or at least be wary of the beginnings of a potential relapse while you are in these situations. Also, write "wiggle room" on the card to remind yourself to cut yourself some slack. If you make a mistake and have a slip one day, get back to your program the next and don't make a big deal out of it. "Wiggle room," or whatever substitute words you come up with, tells you that those slip calories won't be your downfall unless you react to the slip by quitting.

Schedule maintenance checkups. Schedule monthly or quarterly maintenance checkups for the next year or two. Use 30 minutes or so to study your food diary and reflect on what foods you are eating, your portion sizes, the times of day that you eat, feelings associated with the meal, and distracting activities. With regular maintenance checkups, you'll identify and correct patterns that can pull you off your program.

Set your 10-pound regain alarm. After you have reached your weight loss goal, make a contract to rededicate yourself to your program if you regain 10 pounds. You may forget all other maintenance tips, but your scale will remind you of this one. This means you must weigh yourself at least twice a month. Some people avoid weigh-ins because they don't want to see the bad news. But the news should not be good or bad; your weight is just a number that provides feedback. Use the number to make changes, not to beat yourself up.

Dial a dietitian. You don't have to do maintenance by yourself. Call a professional, who can advise you on your diet and meal planning. You can find a registered dietitian in the Yellow Pages, through your doctor, at a hospital, or by contacting the American Dietetic Association.

Read and reap the benefits. Make it a goal to read three or four books a year on exercise and weight management. (You have almost finished one already, that's one down for this year.) Also, subscribe to magazines that publish articles on good nutrition and exercise and recipes. These are my personal trainers. I'm inspired every time I pick up a book or health magazine. You should see my living room, bedroom, and backpack. Every month, inspirational stories and helpful reminders help me with maintenance.

Log on. Weight management sites offer daily inspirational messages, recipes, meal plans, food shopping lists, self-tests, chat-room support, and articles on nutrition. You can anonymously give your age, weight, and other specifics to a virtual dietitian to receive personalized nutrition advice. Sites vary in quality and cost, so check around. Here are a few: CyberDiet.com (www.cyberdiet.com), LEARN—The LifeStyle Company (www.thelifestylecompany.com), eDiets.com (www.ediets.com), DietWatch (www.dietwatch.com), and DietSmart (www.dietsmart.com). Weight Watchers International is also branching out with an interactive Web service.

Review why you want to exercise. Go back to the beginning of the book and review your reasons for exercising. Do they still apply? Revise your list and keep it current by checking it monthly. That review will make maintenance easier.

Keep moving. By this, I mean keep up the daily mall walking—and keep your body working. Too often in maintenance programs, people begin to go through the motions of exercise but not work out with enough oomph! You need to walk briskly to get a good workout.

"Wash your mind out with soap." Remember when your mom caught you swearing as a kid, and she threatened to "wash your mouth out with soap"? She wanted you to watch your mouth and not pick up a swearing habit. Well, I want you to watch your *mind*. Think what you really want to say to yourself, and then say what you really want to hear. Praise yourself often. Develop affirmations and use them daily. Don't be a perfectionist, avoid all-or-nothing thinking, and be positive about your maintenance program. You can do it!

Join a mall walking club. Okay, this suggestion may seem a bit self-serving, but maintenance is a whole lot easier when you have help from your friends and family. Social support is built into mall walking clubs, so join and find a buddy or two. You will keep each other going.

And You're Off!

Congratulations on completing the WalkSport Fit Forever Program! The success you've had at making mall walking and weight management part of your lifestyle is yours and yours alone—you did the work, you put in the time, and now you're reaping the benefits, which you will continue to stockpile as long as you stick with the program!

There's no denying that you've changed over the course of reading this book. This change means growth, and growth means endings and beginnings. Living a new lifestyle may not always go exactly the way you want, but at this point, I am confident that you've experienced enough pleasurable gains to inspire you to keep going—on to the next step and the next and the next. This is fun, this is healthy, and this is you!

WalkSport America's motto is "Let's Get America Walking!" We know the health changes that can come about when Americans walk regularly. So, we ask for your help: Call your neighbors, friends, coworkers, siblings, anyone you know who has not yet found their way to great health. Ask them to join you for a walk—for the good of their health and yours. Imagine what would happen if five people who read this book converted five couch potatoes into regular mall walkers, and then those five converted five more, and on and on—we could start a revolution!

You can do this! Keep up the good work. I'll see you at the mall!

Resources for Walkers

Walking Gadgets

Gadgets can turn a ho-hum workout into a motivating, fun experience. Here is buying information for some of my favorite mall walking gadgets.

Baby Björn Baby Carrier
This soft front carrier allows parents to tote the munchkin along for a walk.
  Price: $80 and up
  Phone: (800) 593-5522 for a store nearest you

Fit Sense FS-1 Speedometer
This device gives you instant feedback while you walk and run, displaying your pace, distance, calories burned, and heart rate. A foot pod on your shoe tracks true speed and distance, not just step count.
  Price: $150 to $299
  Phone: (800) 419-3667
  Web site: www.fitsense.com

Heart Rate Monitor
These gadgets keep track of your heart rate by resting against your chest, under your clothing. While you walk, your heart rate reads out on the "watch."
  Price: $69 and up
  Phone (888) 972-WALK
  Web site: www.walkerswarehouse.com
  Enter code WS0602 for a WalkSport 10% discount.

Optimus AM/FM/TV-Sound/Weather Receiver
Designed for the "active lifestyle," this pocket-size radio that has TV and weather channel options has an earphone jack. Don't wait to walk because you might miss your favorite TV show—listen to it while you walk!
  Price: About $70
  Web site: www.radioshack.com

PowerBelt

This belt attaches around your waist and features a pulley system that works your arms as you pump while you walk. Great for upper-body toning.

Price: About $60
Phone (888) 972-WALK
Web site: www.walkerswarehouse.com
Enter code WS0602 for a WalkSport 10% discount.

Simple Step Counters

I love these, not only for how they measure my mall walks but also for how they give me a snapshot of my movement the remainder of the day. (And what an eye-opener to see how little exercise I get during my normal workday sitting at my desk!) I've found step counters to be such great motivators to remind myself to keep moving that I started to sell them.

Price: About $26
Phone: (800) 757-WALK
Web site: www.walksport.com

Tally Counter

This gadget keeps count of how many laps you've made around the mall. Hold it in the palm of your hand and click for each lap.

Price: About $10
Phone: (800) 338-6337
Web site: www.sportline.com

Walking Poles

Similar to ski poles but with rubber tips, these are great for hiking outside and walking inside, increasing stability, evening weight distribution (saving your knees), and giving you a more efficient workout.

Price: About $70
Phone: (888) 972-WALK
Web site: www.walkerswarehouse.com
Enter code WS0602 for a WalkSport 10% discount.

Walking Gear

Try some of these sites for the best walking gear.

Athleta.com: Women's fitness clothing
www.athleta.com

Fitness Zone: Fitness equipment, treadmills, bikes, and related gear
www.fitnesszone.com

Junonia: Women's active wear for plus-size women
www.junonia.com

New Balance: Wide selection of walking products
www.newbalance.com/productbrowser/walking.html

REI: Complete outdoor sporting, camping, and hiking gear
www.rei.com

Road Runner Sports: Clothing, shoes, and nutritional products
www.roadrunnersports.com

Title Nine Sports: Women's fitness clothing
www.title9sports.com

Volks-Ware: Clothing catalog and walking event guide
www.volks-ware.com

Walking Organizations

One of the most gratifying things about working with walkers is seeing the connections they make with each other, inside *and* outside the mall. If you're looking to spread your wings, or just get started, look up some of these organizations.

American Hiking Society
1422 Fenwick Lane
Silver Spring, MD 20910
(301) 565-6704
(301) 565-6714 (fax)
Web site: www.americanhiking.org
 The American Hiking Society lists about 150 hiking clubs dedicated to keeping and maintaining foot trails in the United States. This organization serves as a resource for locating hiking clubs, trails, and events in your area.

American Volkssport Association (AVA)
1001 Pat Booker Road, Suite 101
Universal City, TX 78148-4147
(800) 830-WALK (hotline)
(210) 659-2112

Web site: www.ava.org

E-mail: AVAHQ@aol.com

The AVA's network of 450 clubs organizes more than 3,000 events per year in all 50 states.

American Walking Association

PO Box 20491

Boulder, CO 80308

(303) 938-9531

E-mail: viisha@attbi.com

This organization features walking camps and training.

North American Racewalking Foundation

PO Box 50312

Pasadena, CA 91115-0312

(626) 441-5459

(626) 799-5106 (fax)

E-mail: NARWF@aol.com

Web site: http://members.aol.com/RWNARF

This organization connects racewalking fans with clubs, coaches, and events. The Web site displays proper racewalking technique through the movements of an animated stick figure.

Rails-to-Trails Conservancy

1100 17th Street, NW, 10th Floor

Washington, DC 20036

(202) 331-9696

(202) 331-9680 (fax)

E-mail: railtrails@transact.org

Web site: www.railtrails.org

This organization helps communities in the United States convert railroad lines into multipurpose public paths. There are about 11,000 miles to lead you through scenic and historic areas.

USA FIT

Web site: www.usafit.com

USA FIT offers a 6-month running and/or walking training program with in-person programs in numerous U.S. cities, or Internet programs for those not in a USA FIT city. All ability levels are welcome.

Walkablock Club of America
Web site: www.walkablock.com
    This club offers members' support in maintaining daily physical activity for long-term health.

Walking for Wellness
NBWHP
600 Pennsylvania Avenue, SE
Suite 310
Washington, DC 20003
(202) 543-9311
(202) 543-9743 (fax)
E-mail: nbwhp@nbwhp.org
Web site: www.nbwhp.org/healthylifestyles
    The Walking for Wellness program is a fitness self-help health awareness and disease prevention program developed by the National Black Women's Health Project (NBWHP). Please note: All program participants are expected to be members of NBWHP.

Walking Web Sites

About.com (Walking)
Web site: www.walking.about.com
    This Web site offers a comprehensive collection of walking-related topics including injury prevention, weight loss, fund-raising walks, and links to a wide range of fitness sites for walkers.

AllWalking.com
Web site: www.allwalking.com
    This site, produced by the editors of the former *Walking* magazine, provides information on walking for fitness, weight loss, and recreation.

The Walking Connection
Web site: www.walkingconnection.com
    This magazine's Web site offers general information about walking and links to sites related to healthy living, walking, and hiking.

Walking Fit on Prevention.com

Web site: www.prevention.com

The Walking Fit section of this site, edited by Maggie Spilner, walking editor of *Prevention* magazine, offers a range of tips on how you can use walking to control your weight and improve your health, buy the right gear, and even find a walking buddy in your town.

The Walking Site

Web site: www.thewalkingsite.com

This Web site offers information about walking clubs, training, motivation, events, and walking gear.

Walking Events

Sometimes the most inspiring way to get motivated is to train for an event—and when you add in a good cause, your walks take on a whole new meaning. Here are some of my favorite nationwide walks.

AIDS Walk

Web site: www.aidswalk.org/finder

According to the *Boston Globe*, this nationwide 5-K or 10-K walk, held at different dates around the country, "is a crucial fund-raiser, but also a celebration, a rededication, an act of remembrance and hope." Find the date for the walk in a city near you.

America's Walk for Diabetes

Web site: www.diabetes.org/walk

At more than 275 sites across the nation, thousands and thousands of walkers are joining the American Diabetes Association in leading the way in the fight against diabetes.

American Heart Walk

(800) AHA-USA1 (or contact your nearest American Heart Association representative)
E-mail: walk@heart.org
Web site: www.americanheart.org

This noncompetitive walking event is geared to companies that form teams of employees, family members, and friends. Most walks are less than 5 miles.

Arthritis Foundation

(800) 283-7800

Web site: www.arthritis.org and click on "Events and Programs"

The Arthritis Walk, a 5-K or 1-mile walk, takes place in the spring. The Jingle Bell Run/Walk is a national fund-raising event, a 5-K fun run or a 5-K fun walk, held in more than 180 cities across the country during November and December. Joints in Motion is the Arthritis Foundation's marathon training program with the goal of raising funds for the Arthritis Foundation. Participants are trained to run or walk a marathon. The program is designed to guide people of all ages and fitness levels through extensive training for this purpose. Approximately 80 percent of all Joints in Motion athletes have never run or walked a marathon before.

Cystic Fibrosis—Great Strides

(800) FIGHT CF

Web site: www.cff.org

This 6.2-mile walk to cure cystic fibrosis is the Cystic Fibrosis Foundation's largest and fastest growing fund-raiser nationwide.

Komen Race for the Cure Series

E-mail: raceforthecure@komen.org

Web site: www.raceforthecure.com

According to their Web site, this is the largest series of 5-K runs/fitness walks in the world. Races are held in more than 100 U.S. cities and three foreign countries with more than 1.3 million participants. Seventy-five percent of the proceeds remain in the local community where the race is held, helping to support breast health education and breast cancer screening and treatment programs for the medically underserved.

Leukemia and Lymphoma Society's Team in Training (TNT)

Web site: www.teamintraining.org

Team in Training is the world's largest endurance sports training program to raise money toward a cure for leukemia, a leading disease killer of children; lymphoma, the leading disease killer of men and women under 35; and other blood-related cancers. Run or walk 26.2 miles, or cycle 100 miles and join the more than 30,000 people who participate on behalf of the Leukemia and Lymphoma Society.

March for Parks

(202) 208-5478 or (800) NAT-PARK, ext. 370

E-mail: jbutts@npca.org

Web site: www.nps.gov/npweek

This nationwide march is run to involve communities in park protection. For more information about March for Parks and National Park Week, please refer to the National Park Service Web site.

March of Dimes

E-mail: walkamerica@marchofdimes.com
Web site: www.walkamerica.org

The "WalkAmerica" event draws almost 500,000 walkers from all 50 states, including 24,000 company teams, to benefit babies born prematurely or with birth defects. It is the March of Dimes' biggest fund-raiser.

MS Challenge Walk

(800) FIGHT MS
Web site: www.nationalmssociety.org/mycommunity

In this 3-day, 50-mile event, participants raise money for vital research and programming dedicated to finding a cure and aiding those who live with multiple sclerosis. Contact your local chapter for information about MS Walks.

Vancouver Discovery Walk Festival

(877) 269-2009
E-mail: info@discoverywalk.org
Web site: www.discoverywalk.org

The Discovery Walk Festival held in Vancouver is a yearly walking festival held in April. It is sponsored by International Walk Fest and the City of Vancouver, Washington. A dozen different nations participate in this event that is sanctioned by the International Marching League.

Walk for Hunger History

Web site: www.projectbread.org

For more than 30 years, Project Bread's Walk for Hunger has provided much-needed resources for hungry people in Massachusetts. The Walk for Hunger is the nation's largest annual 1-day fund-raiser to address local hunger.

The Walk to Cure Diabetes

Web site: www.jdrf.org/support/walk_to_cure.php

This walkathon is held in 186 locations throughout the year benefiting the Juvenile Diabetes Research Foundation. More than 400,000 men, women, and children—including those from 5,000 large corporations and local companies, along with 3,500 family teams—participate each year. In 2001, the Walk raised more than $70 million for diabetes research.

Index

Boldfaced page references indicate illustrations. Underscored page references indicate boxed text.

Southdale Shopping Center, 9, 31
walker-friendly, 15–17
Mall walking. *See also* Arthritis, mall walking
and; Personal experiences of mall
walking; Pregnancy and mall walking
with children, 90–91, 198–202
communities, 27–28
depression prevention and, <u>113</u>
elders as role models for, 158–59
etiquette, 21, 24–26
family support in
importance of, 171–73
for pregnant walkers, 196–98
general benefits of, 10–11, 13–15
health benefits of, 32–36
movement, 9–10
personal motivation for, <u>92</u>
safety issues, 14, 192–95
scheduling, 91
in smoke-free zones, 92
starting program, 26–27
weight management and, 10
yielding to shoppers and, 25
yoga and, 171
Meat and legumes food group, 51 52
Mental edge
avoiding all-or-nothing thinking, 150–51
avoiding perfectionism, 151, 154–55
preventing staleness, 147–50
setbacks and
avoiding, 145–47
managing, 155–56
personal experience of, <u>146–47</u>
"talking back" excuses and, <u>149</u>
Metabolism and weight loss, 54–55
Mid-meal break, 164
Milk food group, 51
Minerals, 43–44
Motivation, personal, <u>92</u>
Muscles
building and strengthening, 33, 36
endurance and, 33
fitness and, 85
flexibility of, 33, 87

N

National Heart, Lung, and Blood Institute
(NHLBI), 68
Negative self-talk, countering, 61–62, <u>63</u>,
154

NHLBI, 68
Niacin, 43
"No pain, no gain" concept, 29, 208
Nutritional building blocks
carbohydrates, 41
dietary fat, 41–42
importance of, 40
minerals, 43–44
protein, 40–41
vitamins, 42–43
water, 44–45

O

Obesity
heart disease and, 7
mortality rate and, 110
risk factors for, 70–71, <u>70</u>
Oils food group, 49–51
Optimism, importance of, 63–66
Overeating, avoiding, <u>155</u>
Overuse injuries, 179–80
Overweight, assessing, 68–69

P

PACE program, 209
Pain, from injury, 179–80
Pain management and mall walking, <u>12–13</u>,
<u>30</u>. *See also* Arthritis, mall walking and
Parking, at mall, 14, 24
Partners, workout, 91, 99, 160–62, <u>161</u>
Patience, adopting, 159
People with Arthritis Can Exercise (PACE)
program, 209
Pep talks, 167–70
Perfectionism, avoiding, 97, 151, 154–55
Personal experiences of mall walking
arthritis, <u>206–7</u>
change, <u>60</u>
depression prevention, <u>113</u>
dining out, <u>181</u>, <u>186–87</u>
family support, <u>172–73</u>
pain management, <u>12–13</u>, <u>30</u>
setbacks, <u>146–47</u>
stress management, <u>12–13</u>, <u>30</u>
weight loss, <u>12–13</u>, <u>104–5</u>, <u>113</u>, <u>186–87</u>
Personal trainers, 180–82
Phosphorus, 44
Pizza, 185

Y

Z